# PARISH RENEWAL
# AT THE GRASSROOTS

# Parish Renewal at the Grassroots

## David Prior

**FRANCIS ASBURY PRESS**
*of Zondervan Publishing House*
Grand Rapids, Michigan

PARISH RENEWAL AT THE GRASSROOTS
is the title of the North American edition of
*The Church in the Home*

Copyright © 1983 by David Prior
First published in 1983 by Marshall Morgan and Scott
Publications Ltd.
Part of the Marshall Pickering Holdings Group
3 Beggarwood Land, Basingstoke, Hants, RG23 7LP, UK
A subsidiary of the Zondervan Corporation

FRANCIS ASBURY PRESS
is an imprint of
Zondervan Publishing House
1415 Lake Drive S.E.
Grand Rapids, Michigan 49506

**Library of Congress Cataloging in Publication Data**

Prior, David, 1940-
      Parish renewal at the grassroots.

      Reprint. Originally published: Church in the home.
Baskingstoke, Hants. : Marshall, Morgan, and Scott., c1983.
      1. Church renewal.  2. House churches.  3. Christian communities.
I. Title.
BV600.2.P74   1987        253.7'6        86-28980
ISBN 0-310-38370-6

*Printed in the United States of America*


87  88  89  90  91  92  93 / EE / 10  9  8  7  6  5  4  3  2  1

# Contents

# Acknowledgements

My debt to countless people is obvious. Special thanks to the staff and people of St. Aldate's Church, Oxford, for giving me time and space to put the churnings of 10 years or so onto paper.

I was able to spend this leave in Costa Rica, a crossroads for Christian traffic of all kinds in Latin America. Amongst the many people in San Jose I want to thank most sincerely are:

Bill Cook, for making patient time to set up a stimulating set of interviews;

Mel & Woody Lovett, for tolerating a writer upstairs;

Tom & Joyce Hanks, for lending me their house; as well as Tom's library;

Pablo Richard, Alberto Barrientos, Fred Tingley and others, for giving me time for talking;

Ricardo Foulkes, for a kind and timely welome.

Several individuals have been of great assistance in uncovering material which I could never have found otherwise, even in the libraries of Oxford — especially:

Derek Winter, Michael Rowe, Jonathan Chao, and other correspondents.

I am also in debt to David Ho Sang, who spent several extra days in Seoul in September 1982 in order to take a look at the Full Gospel Central Church. His wife, Betty, has deciphered my scrawl and reduced it to printed form with patience, aplomb and cheerfulness — thank you very much.

But my beloved wife, Rosemary, together with our four children (Marcus, Daniel, Emma and Susanna), must come first. They put up with my meanderings to and fro, particularly in 1982, with graciousness, utter loyalty and understanding. They are the church in our home.

# Foreword

This is a fascinating book of considerable importance for the western church today. Most Christians readily acknowledge the present-day malaise of the church, but few offer any constructive suggestions for effective renewal. This book is both radical and biblical, historical and contemporary, and focuses on the essential dynamic behind every significant growth of the church since the days of the New Testament.

A few years ago I read a comparatively small booklet by David Prior on the same theme. I found that booklet so stimulating that I urged him to expand the material into a book for the benefit of the wider church. I am delighted with this result.

The last decade has seen the mushrooming of house groups all over this country, and indeed throughout the world. In these gatherings Christians meet to share their faith; but even when these are encouraged by local church leaders, many home meetings are little more than Bible study or prayer groups. Often, however, even these groups are not encouraged by the clergy who feel threatened by them. Many Christians therefore, feel frustrated by the conservatism of church leaders, have broken away from the mainline denominations and have formed independent churches — commonly called 'the house church movement', of which there are several quite distinct strands — thus dividing the body of Christ still further.

The biblical norm, maintains David Prior, is the church in the home. He is rightly critical of the breakaway and independent 'house church', but presses for the home groups to become consciously the church in that place whilst remaining firmly within the parish of a mainline denomination. He sees the church in the home as something far more significant than a Bible study group or prayer meeting. It should be in every sense 'the church' expressed by worship and prayer, word and sacrament, fellowship and evangelism, service and mission. However small a home church may be, its members should look for the full range of spiritual gifts and ministries to emerge for its healthy growth.

The value and strength of this book is to be found not only in the biblical basis that David Prior gives for all this, but in the rich material he draws from the church in Third World countries, notably Latin America. It is here, as well as in Korea, Uganda, China, Hungary and Russia, that we find extraordinary church growth today — amongst those who are materially poor but spiritually rich. As Prior rightly maintains, we in the affluent west should not only give generously to our poorer brethren, but humbly receive from them vital lessons for spiritual life and growth. He therefore gives much valuable detail of the remarkable 'grassroots communities' of Latin America, which by their whole lifestyle are highly prophetic for the rest of the church today. Here are principles that are relevant both for depressed inner-city areas, for middle-class suburban churches, and for rural communities.

If we could act upon the lessons of this book we would see the healthiest spiritual revolution in this country since the Wesleyan revival in the eighteenth century. It would be a revolution actively involving every Christian without becoming independent of the traditional churches, and a revolution creatively bringing to our modern society the powerful influence of the kingdom of God.

I am profoundly grateful to God for this fresh vision of the church in the home, and hope that it will point the way for today's church in this critical generation.

*David Watson*

# Introduction

## Long dissatisfaction

Three major factors have brought this book into being. First, *dissatisfaction* over a long period of time with existing church structures — a feeling of disenchantment which most Christians experience with varying degrees of intensity. The wineskins rarely seem suitable for the new wine of God's grace in Jesus Christ. Most church structures bring atrophy rather than growth, stunting the creativity and the longings which the Holy Spirit plants in God's people. They also divide the family of God by pandering to the peer-group priorities of the secular world, instead of demonstrating the exciting reality of genuine oneness in Christ. Because our present structures both deaden and divide, they also drive away many Christians who want and ought to be properly integrated into local churches, but who find existing patterns of church life stifling and unattractive.

## Steady disillusionment

Secondly, the virtually universal phenomenon of small groups has not really produced local churches worth the name. So *disillusionment* with the widespread proliferation of such groups is a major factor in searching for something different. This is in no sense to decry the real benefits which individuals have undoubtedly received as members of prayer groups, fellowship groups, Bible-study groups, etc. It is simply to underline their inadequacy in terms of discovering what a local church is intended by God to become. This failure may well be due to their attempt to meet felt needs rather than any response to divine imperatives. These human needs are threefold[1] — 'the need to be', i.e. to feel authentically human;

9

'the need to belong' to some group; and 'the need to have and to do' — the human need for a sense of destiny and purpose.[1]

## Restless hankering

Authentic human needs can be adequately met only in response to God's own imperatives. This inner conviction, which is essentially a biblical perspective, forced me back to the New Testament picture of the church for more authoritative and creative patterns of Christian growth. It has always been very obvious that the church, as the community of the Holy Spirit, must be God's arena for meeting such fundamental human needs — not little parts of the church, but the church as such. It does not require much imagination or expertise to appreciate that the church began its life in people's homes — and that basic fact stayed with me from the first time it struck my consciousness. Ever since, I have known in my bones that 'the church in the home' must be the way forward. This *restless hankering* for something better, something from God, is the third factor behind this book.

## South Africa

In the Cape Town, *South Africa*, parish where my wife and I worked for over seven years, we were able to break down the congregation into what we called 'House Churches'. This process began in 1974 with two. Eight years later, there are about 50. They have fluctuated immensely in both vitality and relevance, but they remain an important clue to the genuine possibility of 'the church in the home'. For most people involved in one of these house churches, it has become the focus of their Christian lives. One family, which had to move overseas for a year, found that their strongest yearning was for the life of their house church — which they came to appreciate far more when separated from it. There have been many pointers in that parish — and in countless other South African churches where similar growth has occurred — which together indicate that this is the right way to go.

## South America

In recent years several other perspectives have been provided through travel, reading and interaction with Christians in other parts of the world. These have been reinforced by studying church history. For example, in 1976 I visited southern Chile, where small communities of (mainly) Mapuche Indians, recently converted to Christ *en masse*, were living out the reality of being the church. Around the same time came an opportunity to spend a fortnight in the congregation of the Hidalgo church in Buenos Aires, *Argentina*, at that stage pastored by Juan Carlos Ortiz.[2] Until that experience, I had not seen (outside residential communities) such a clear example of Christian love in action through thorough commitment to one another and sharing the whole of life together in small groups. There was clearly something more to be discovered.

## Zimbabwe and Uganda

Two visits to African countries going through the agonies of civil war produced another perspective — *Zimbabwe* in 1979 and *Uganda* in 1981. In both countries there is a large number of active Christians. These men and women have been through — and continue to experience — intense suffering because of the violence let loose in their community over many years. Their resilience has been truly remarkable. One simple factor above all others stood out — it was often too dangerous for Christians to meet together in large church buildings: the streets were full of violence. It was, however, possible to meet with other Christians in the same street or just around the corner. In fact, such home churches were not, to my knowledge, actually in existence. One of the reasons was — in Uganda at least — a heavy emphasis and reliance on the clergyman. Time and time again we will have to come back to this factor. In both Zimbabwe and Uganda Christian leaders, with whom I spent time in discussion, saw immediately the priority of building up home churches, mainly for the very pragmatic reason that the immediate situation virtually required it.

## China

Where it is actually illegal for large congregations to gather in church buildings, except under very severe restrictions and in circumstances which encourage nominal religion, home churches have become the *only* way for Christians to meet and visibly be the church. From *China* in 1980 comes the following cameo: 'In most places in rural Zhejiang Province church meetings are held in homes, because most of the church buildings have been borrowed by the communes. Some churches have been turned into factories. But because the people are so many and the houses are small, even where some places are big, they are very crowded. The people aren't afraid of difficulties. They come from great distances for meetings, and stay until 11 o'clock at night before returning. Even if they have to walk one or two hours, they don't mind.' Evidence from other provinces of China indicates similar happenings in many parts of the country.[3]

## Hungary

Similar facts emerge from behind the Iron Curtain. In *Hungary*, for example, 'there are probably about 4,000 small groups of 10–15 persons, mostly young, who meet in their homes to discuss religious or human problems and to celebrate the Eucharist. These groups gradually form communities which give each other assistance in the problems of day-to-day living. While the official Church is gathering scarcely any converts, these groups contain people who have been brought up without religion.'[4]

## Russia

A variation on the same theme is provided in the 'Christian Seminars' in *Russia,* where young Orthodox Christians have been gathering in small groups in Moscow since 1974. These 'seminars' have four goals:

(i) To establish a fraternal Christian relationship of love. . . . 'It is our desire that the faith we have acquired and the liberty that flows from it should find outward expression in the creation of an independent Christian community not subject to the control of the State.'

(ii) To develop an Orthodox view of the world and to acquire theological training. . . . 'We have, in general, grown up in families that were atheist or without religion . . . we need to be able to listen attentively, responsibly and continually to what is happening in the world; and we need to be inserted into its future in a concrete religious fashion.'

(iii) To become involved in active missionary witness. . . . 'We must bring the joyous influence of the Gospel into every sphere of human relationship.

(iv) To defend religious freedom in the U.S.S.R. and the rights of believers. . . . 'We maintain that, in defending the independence of the Church we are defending man himself, the meaning and dignity of his existence.'

It is not surprising to discover that the founder of these Christian Seminars, Alexandre Ogorodnikov, and other principal members are at present in prison or else being subjected to forced medical treatment in a psychiatric hospital.[5] In spite of this persecution, it is believed that such a network of little communities will enable the church in Russia to bear up under the strongest pressures from the State. It could never be eliminated; indeed, there would gradually emerge 'a community of communities' of great solidarity and effectiveness.

## Singapore and Korea

From other, less pressurised, parts of the world come reports of similar expressions of home church life. In Asia, two significant examples can be found in Singapore and Korea. In *Singapore,* where land is at a premium and buildings consequently spread upwards in high-rise apartment-blocks, there has been a growing commitment to home churches, sometimes on several different floors of an apartment-block. In *Korea* a church has sprung up which must break all known records for sheer numerical growth — the Full Gospel Central Church in Seoul. Between the early 1960's and 1982, this church has grown to an active membership of nearly 250,000. It is structurally based on 'home cell units' which together 'form a scriptural system based on biblical precepts.' They are

seen, not as causing growth, but as being channels for growth
— 'the positive principles present in the cell system create a
channel for phenomenal spiritual and numerical growth.
Most importantly, the cell system builds into its members a
therapeutic lifestyle that brings healing of the body, mind and
spirit to those involved.'[6] This Korean church is so remarkable that we will need to return to it later for closer investigation. For the present, it is worth noting that it is the most
vibrant example we can find of a large congregation basing its
whole life on home churches in this cellular pattern.


## Latin America

Africa, South America, Russia, China, Hungary, Singapore,
Korea — all over the world the Holy Spirit is manifestly
moving in similar, but distinctive, ways. And yet there is one
other phenomenon which, I believe, transcends all these
examples in potential, relevance and challenge. It is a movement located mainly in Latin America amongst Roman
Catholics, although it is now springing up in many other parts
of the world. In Latin American countries it is also bringing
Catholics and Protestants together. The movement has been
given several names, both by those trying to describe it and by
those who are part of it. 'Basic Christian Communities' is one
description, taken from the Spanish — 'communidades de
base'. The most evocative and accurate description is 'grassroots communities', and we will use this title throughout the
book.

What are these grassroots communities? They are 'small
groups of about 10 to 30 people from the same area and same
class who come together to discuss concrete problems in the
light of the Bible, and to discuss lines of action in response to
their situation. The overwhelming majority are poor and
come from the margins of society.'[7] '. . . They find room to
exist, to think, to pray, to meet, to plan, to dream.'[7a] If these
descriptions sound like any Bible study group in some English
or American church, then let us examine the way members of
these grassroots communities see their life together: for example, at a gathering of members in Vitoria, Brazil, in 1975, one

question was put: What kind of grassroots community do we want?'

(i) 'We want mature Christian communities that are committed to Christ, and to the people and their liberation.'

(ii) 'We want communities that are led by the gifts of the Spirit, and that are integrated into the total church, along with other communities, in a spirit of free and fraternal intercommunication.'

(iii) 'We desire communities that are in a constant process of reflection and of growth, in-depth, under firm leadership.'[8]

Let the grassroots communities continue to speak for themselves: 'For us, a grassroots community must be open, global, inclusive of all the elements in the church. It cannot be limited to a group; it must be the *normal* community of a baptized person, and so anyone has the right to belong, if he or she has been baptized. . . . The charismatic movement can create a good climate, can awaken gospel values, but it remains just a movement. It forms a prayer group, a mutual-help group, but do not call that a grassroots community. In Latin America there exist groups and movements which help the forward thrust of our church, or do not help it, or even hamper it: for they centralise too much the persons around the goals of the movement, and forget a little bit the totality of the church where we all ought to meet, even if we are different or follow different movements.'[9]

Quite simply, these grassroots communities *ARE* the church in that place — not part of the church, or a group within or on the outskirts or even outside the church, but the church. This is precisely the definition members themselves adopt; 'We are the church.' Even Pope John Paul II told the Brazilian bishops that the grassroots communities are 'true local churches' — a comment made public by Antonio Fragoso, bishop of the Diocese of Crateus in North-East Brazil, where remarkable growth has taken place.

It is estimated that there were over 150,000 such communities in Latin America in 1982, half of which were in Brazil. They are to be found in both rural and urban situations, especially in the 'favelas' (shanty-towns) which sprawl around virtually every city in Latin America. They are often encouraged with great enthusiasm by the Catholic hierarchy (i.e.

parish priests and diocesan bishops); sometimes they are merely tolerated; in many places they are squashed. Where they are integrated into the life of a parish, they often become the warp and woof of its life. There are examples of a whole diocese being organized through grassroots communities. As well as Brazil, they can be found in strength in Chile, Colombia, Mexico, Nicaragua, Honduras, Guatemala.

Of course, to give the name 'church' to these communities by itself signifies nothing. The crucial fact is that they not only see themselves as the church and are called such by those in ecclesiastical authority, but also live out their life together as microcosms of the church. The sheer exuberance of this experience is caught in this statement by another "articulator-from-within" of the grassroots communities.

'Other churches may be richer in institutions, or talk more about the Gospel. But the grassroots communities are more evangelical because of the evangelical notes of joy, hope, enthusiasm, joviality, largeness of heart, good news despite oppression, and the certainty of victory despite evident obstacles. The new figure of the church is born when poor and unprepossessing groups of Christians gather together, even under a mango tree, to pray, to hear the Gospel, to witness to their faith in Jesus and to follow Him.'[10]

One final statement from within the communities themselves will suffice to underline their justified self-awareness as being the church:

'They are *not a movement*, an association or a religious congregation. . . . They are *not a method* (or the only method) of building up the church: they are the church itself. They are *not a miraculous* recipe for all the ills of society and the church. They are the church renewing itself. . . . A pilgrim people and perhaps a sinful one, yet on the move with Jesus and the Spirit. . . . They are *not a Utopia*: they are a sign of the Kingdom, though they are not the Kingdom. . . . They are *not messianic*, but they can be prophetic and produce prophets like the church should. They are *not a natural . . . community . . .* identified with a race, language, people, family. . . . They are the church . . . in many countries, a force for unity between different races, lanuages, cultures. They are *not a protest group*, although their life is a protest against the mediocrity, sloth and inauthenticity of many. . . . They are *not special groups for special people*. They are the church committed to the ordinary man, to the poor, to those who suffer injustice. . . . They are *not closed*: they are open to dialogue with all. They are *not a reform of anything* in pastoral work: they are a decisive pastoral option made in order to construct a new image of the church. It may appear quite harmless to say that the grassroots community is the church. But precisely because it is the church itself, it is a very dangerous thing, because the church is dangerous: it is a revolutionary leaven in history, reconstructing the world with Christ's values and standards.'[11]

Hopefully enough has been said to show the exciting significance of the grassroots communities. When put alongside what God is doing in other parts of the world today, these facts force us to ask many questions of the way our church life is organized. In particular, Chistians in the West, notably in Europe, need to learn as much as possible from such divine initiatives in other countries and cultures.

## Church history

In addition, even a scant reading of church history brings to our attention the different occasions on which similar events took place under the inspiration of the Holy Spirit — e.g. in 6th century Ireland, *St Patrick* and his successors developed grassroots communities which were perfectly suited to the village organisation of the Celtic tribes of the region. In the 13th century, *St Francis* gathered around him those who would together live the life of Jesus and proclaim the Gospel by example and preaching. The revolutionary actions of the *Lollards* in 15th century England took to its logical conclusion the radical biblical preaching of John Wycliffe. Better known are the 'class-meetings' and 'bands' of *John Wesley*'s discipling methods. The relevance of grassroots community life for authentic Christian discipleship, for bold and effective evangelism, for courageous confrontation of injustice, has frequently been underlined throughout the history of the church.

## The Bible

Wherever the Bible has been taken seriously, such grassroots phenomena have occurred. One of the most important catalysts in the Latin American situation has been the unprecedented availability of the Scriptures in popular Spanish — the result of a specific decision by the Catholic Church at Vatican II about 20 years ago. For the first time, the ordinary people in the Catholic Chuch have been able to discover for themselves the true message of Jesus and the Kingdom of God. It would be excessively naive — and wrong — to attribute the life of the grassroots communities simply to reading the Bible. Nevertheless, one of Central America's most authoritative spokesmen and enablers of the grassroots communities, Dr. Pablo Richard (an exiled Chilean), quietly but firmly described the movement in Latin America as 'a new Reformation of the Catholic Church.'

Protestant churches with access to the Scriptures in their own language for generations have not exactly blazed a trail in demonstrating the truth and beauty of body-life in Christ. Indeed, one of the intriguing facets of the Protestant Reformation is the way its major personalities — especially *Luther and Calvin* — perceived the need for such committed Christian community-life, but did not pursue it. In fact, both Luther and Calvin had its importance impressed upon them from an early stage. Calvin almost certainly attended secret Huguenot 'conventicles' while a student in Paris in the 1520's, while Luther expressed his own conviction that, 'those who seriously want to be Christians and to confess the gospel in deed and word would have to register their names and gather themselves somewhere in a house alone. . . . Here one could also conduct baptism and communion in a brief and fine manner, and direct everything to the word, prayer and mutual love. . . . In brief, if one had the people who earnestly desired to be Christians, the order and manner could quickly be brought about.' This was clearly Luther's own heart's desire, but he felt compelled to continue: 'However, I cannot and do not wish yet to set up or to organize such a congregation, for I do not yet have the people for it. I do not see many who ask for such a thing. But if it comes that I must do it and am compelled, so that I cannot with good conscience leave it undone, then I shall gladly do my part in it, and give the best help I can.'[12]

## The House Church Movement

By this time it must be clear that the theme of this book is not the House Church movement, as it has come to be known, in the U.K. or U.S.A. These House Churches have grown as a protest against the formalism and deadness of much traditional church life, and they exist over against the mainline churches, not as another expression of their existence. We are to examine 'a new way of being the church' (one of the self-descriptions frequently used by the grassroots communities in Latin America). In addition, we are not concerned with such communities in isolation one from another, but as they together express the life of a local church. Most radical movements of this kind (either in response to sterility and opposition or in a spirit of independence, or both) have in the past left the mainstream and formed a new church, as today's House Churches are doing. Fired by the refusal of the grassroots communities[12a] to take this route, existing churches could well begin to respond to the divine imperative with radical restructuring along the lines of the church in the home. It might even happen that, what the Anabaptist movement in the 16th century failed to achieve in its attempts to bring radical reformation of church structures and community-life, as well as reformation of doctrine and practice, this 'new Reformation' in Latin America will actually pioneer and promote throughout the Roman Catholic Church, and throughout the worldwide church.

## The Church in the home

'We need to develop small churches within existing congregational and denominational frameworks, and to make them the basic unit of church life.'[13] Such an approach will necessarily involve a radical re-think about existing structures and organisations in a local church. Many groups and meetings will have to be terminated, if only to make time and space for this more fundamental and comprehensive way of being the church. This is, in effect, what the Conference of Latin American Bishops indicated at Medellin, Colombia, in 1973, when they called the grassroots communities 'the first and fundamental ecclesial nucleus . . . the initial cell of the ecclesiastical structures.'[14]

Are we prepared to walk this road today? The purpose of this book is to motivate Christians to begin, to persevere with, this journey. Kindling a vision of what God desires and can accomplish needs to be grounded in what He is already doing. For this reason, I propose to make full use of a remarkable document (reproduced in full as Appendix A) from Vitoria in Brazil. Entitled 'The Church the People Want', it was written by members of local grassroots communities as guidelines for each community. Throughout the archdiocese of Vitoria, the church is divided into grassroots communities. Each chapter heading is taken from this document, together with a brief quotation which conveys the gist of each theme. The sheer truth, power and beauty expressed in the document can best be appreciated by absorbing this description of the kind of area in which these people live:

'In a Vitoria *favela*, people live in shacks built on stilts above a swamp divided by an open sewer, which carries the effluent of a hospital built on a hill half a mile away. The local authority is filling in the swamp by dumping garbage, so that effectively people are living in the middle of a rubbish tip — a fact for which some at least are grateful, since rubbish suitably sifted can be recycled and used for household effects.'[15]

In such situations the Lord is building His church. No wonder 'Hell's foundations quiver.'

# CHAPTER ONE

# A tiny diamond

*'It is better to be bothered about quality rather than quantity: a tiny diamond is far more valuable than a lorryload of stones. . . . We are only concerned with small communities made up of people who know they are the church. It is with these that we are going to set about the work of spreading the gospel. . . .'*[1]

It is now generally recognized that the church in apostolic times gathered in the homes of believers, and that any proper understanding of its worship, teaching, fellowship, mission and ministry must come from that perspective. This situation continued into the third century. It seems probable that the normal situation in a town or city in the Mediterranean world was for several Christian homes in the area to become the focus for the gathered life of the church. For example, Aquila and Priscilla seem to have hosted 'the church in their house' in three cities — Corinth, Ephesus and Rome.[2] Each home church had its identity and distinctive life, but there were occasions when 'the whole church' in a city would come together.[3] Equally, it was possible to call together 'the elders' of the church in one particular place for a special purpose.[4]

Obviously the numbers in any home church would, to a large extent, depend on the size of the home. 'The entertaining-room in a moderately well-to-do household could hold around thirty people comfortably.'[5] Such large homes were by no means the only, or even the major, focus for church life in the first century. Within a few weeks of Pentecost, there were well over 10,000 believers meeting 'from household to household' throughout Jerusalem — and that is a conservative figure, based on the actual numbers quoted by Luke and making due allowance for those pilgrims who would have been visiting the city specifically for the feast of Pentecost.[6] Perhaps the most remarkable fact about the church in Jerusalem was its unity — 'the company of those who believed were of one heart and soul.'[7] Sheer numbers and the absence of any large building in which they could meet both indicate that their unity was given by the Spirit. The disciples were meeting in numerous home churches, but there was a strong commitment to one another as Christians and a manifest inter-dependence.

## Small is beautiful

When this portrait is put together, we see a Christian community with distinctive, but familiar, dynamics — they were closely linked with one another in small home churches, but they also experienced the strength of being a large witnessing community. E.F. Schumacher, author of the book *Small is Beautiful*, has written:

'In the affairs of men, there always appears to be a need for at least two things simultaneously which, on the face of it, seem to be incompatible and to exclude one another. We always need both freedom and order. We need the freedom of lots and lots of small autonomous units and, at the same time, the orderliness of large-scale . . . unity and co-ordination. When it comes to action, we obviously need small units, because action is a highly personal affair, and one cannot be in touch with more than a very limited number of persons at one time . . . or to put it differently, it is true that all men are brothers, but it is also true that in our active personal relationships we can, in fact, be brothers to only a few of them, and we are called upon to show more brotherliness to them than we could possibly show to the whole of mankind.'[8]

Thus, human needs are met in response to the divine imperative to the church to be both small and larger. The larger identity, though mathematically the sum total of the small units, in fact has more spiritual power than simply adding the resources of one home church to other home churches — in rather the same way as a well-coordinated team is stronger than the sum of its individual talents. However, the church in an area will be stunted to the extent that any believers are not committed to one another in a home church. As the people of Vitoria say, 'We are only concerned with small communities made up of people who know they are the church. It is with these that we are going to set about the work of spreading the gospel.'

## Marxism

The fundamental human need to belong in a small group of this kind has been maximised and manipulated by Marxism. It is no coincidence that the most widespread and challenging examples of the home church are to be found in countries dominated or severely threatened by Communism. Their cell-system is an obvious counterfeit of the home church. It is arguable that Communism would never have succeeded so spectacularly, if the Christian church had responded to the divine imperative to be the church. That was certainly the view of Emil Brunner:

'It is because the Church has neglected in almost all ages to create a true fellowship in Christ that we are confronted by the phenomenon of modern Communism . . . With or without the churches, if necessary even in opposition to them, God will cause the *ecclesia* to become a real community of brothers.'[9]

This statement of confidence in God's own determination to build His church needs to be heard. At times the sheer emptiness of church meetings causes despair, if not desperation. The very essence of the church is meeting God and meeting one another. Without the smallness of the home church, such genuine meeting will always be at the mercy of endless meetings.

## Scottish Highlands

Examples of Christians opting for structures which truly do promote encounter with God and with one another can be found throughout the history of the church — often in the most unexpected places. The rise and establishment of the Fellowship Meeting in the Scottish Highlands towards the end of the eighteenth century is a case in point. 'The great object of the fellowship meeting was the mutual comfort and edification of believers . . . How was it conducted? The minister presides and, after prayer, praise and the reading of a portion of Scripture, he calls on any one who is anxious to propose a question to do so. This call is responded to by some man who rises and mentions a passage of Scripture describing some feature of the Christian character. . . . The scope of the passage is then opened up by the minister, who calls by name on such as are of repute for piety, experience and gifts to 'speak the question'. One after another rises and . . . speaks from the heart what he has felt, and feared, and enjoyed under the power of the truth. Thereafter the minister sums up all that has been said, correcting, confirming and expanding, as may be necessary. . . . The person who proposed the question is then usually called to engage in prayer and, with praise and benediction, the meeting is closed.'[10]

The spiritual life engendered within and out of these fellowship meetings is well documented: 'They loved one another. . . . Sometimes differences would arise, but they were felt by them all as a family affliction would be felt. In such cases a peacemaker would always be found.' One, John Munro of Kiltearn, came across a brother in desperate poverty in the depths of winter. He at once hurried to every Christian within reach and 'in the morning of the morrow, horses laden with creels full of provisions, began to arrive at the empty house in Arbol, and before that day closed a supply of meat, butter and cheese was stored up in it that sufficed for a year and a day.'[11] The comments of John Kennedy on the vital importance of these meetings, written as they were in 1861, are particularly striking: 'So naturally do such meetings arise out of a healthful state of religious feeling that the communities in which they are awanting are those from whom an apology is required.'[12]

There is an invaluable insight here — such home churches cannot be imposed on a dead congregation; they are the inevitable overflow of spiritual life. The converse is also true: where there is no such encounter in Christ with one another, it is questionable whether there is authentic spiritual life in that congregation. And if there is such life, it is likely to stagnate and evaporate. On the other hand, the experience of grassroots communities in Latin America makes it very plain that such life cannot be manipulated into being. 'What can and should happen is that the institution provide the space for life from below and give it freedom to develop.'[13] This willingness on the part of those in leadership to respond to the initiatives of the Holy Spirit lies at the heart of the matter.

## A threat to the clergy

For many pastors and ministers, including bishops and archbishops, such home church life is very threatening. The reasons for this fear are profound and manifold. Clergy have not been trained to operate in this way. Orthodoxy in doctrine is usually seen to be of prime importance, and such home churches look like potential seedbeds of heresy. The human need to control situations for which we are held responsible becomes very urgent. There is, moreover, a crisis of identity and role amongst most clergy today. For many, uncomfortable experience of small groups in the past obstructs openness to the Spirit now. Even when scope is given for this pattern of church life, it is very tempting to keep tight control even while decentralising and delegating. To many clergy, delegation looks and feels like abdication, especially when the actual teething troubles begin. Hopefully, the thrust of Scripture, coupled with further examples from church history and contemporary Christian experience, will bring greater confidence to respond to the creative Spirit of God. The comment of the parish priest in Portezuelo in the Diocese of Chillan, Chile, is refreshing:

'The grassroots communities in Portezuelo sprung up due to the bursting forth of the Creator Spirit in this corner of the world. They are not the fruit of a scientific design or formula, but rather of the dynamic action of the Spirit who forms the family of God despite so many human limitations and shortcomings.'[14]

The Portezuelo example is one of the most encouraging we have come across. The parish is made up of 18 rural Christian communities spread out over a large area. The smallest grassroots community has some 14 families. The larger ones have as many as eighty people at a gathering. A team of eight mature Christians (three schoolteachers and five peasants) continually visit and 'animate' the communities. The parish priest co-ordinates this pastoral care, acts as a focus for the parish, visits each community three times a year, and generally enables the gifts and ministries within the body of Christ. The maturity of this parish's spiritual life has led to the bishop asking it to take responsibility for work in other parts of the diocese. This has happened three times in the last seven years, leading to the formation of grassroots communities in all three areas. In addition, the Portezuelo region has been immensely enriched by the way the Christian communities have launched themselves into many areas of social need: the list of such projects successfully initiated by Christians working together, and today under the aegis mainly of local or central government, is impressive — a resident doctor at the local hospital; a nurse and midwife for outlying areas; three rural clinics; a local crafts centre; a fire-fighting brigade; running water; and a centre for rehabilitation of alcoholics. No wonder the priest says: 'The Holy Spirit has been the heart and soul of all that has happened here.'[15]

## Home cells in Korea

John Hurston helped in the early days of the vast Full Gospel Central Church in Seoul Korea, and is now responsible for the church's outreach to train pastors from different parts of the world in the principles of church growth. He affirms that the concept of 'home cell units' requires that 'a church already has the vital elements of prayer, faith and enthusiastic testimony.'[16] Given these three realities by the Holy Spirit, any congregation is ready to base its life on home churches. Hurston describes home cell units as a channel for growth, not a cause of growth — an important distinction. He sees them as a channel for six things: for releasing people into love, both towards God and one another; for providing effective pastoral care; for developing a continuing appetite for God's Word; for releasing clear personal testimony to Jesus the Lord; for reinforcing the priorities and practices of the whole church fellowship; and for encouraging regular personal evangelism amongst friends, colleagues, family and neighbours.[17]

If such home cell units, or home churches, have the capacity to channel such torrents of spiritual life, it is worth discovering (clergy and people together) what then becomes of the ministry of the person set apart by ordination to serve the people of God. This will become clearer as we proceed, but for the time being let us hear the words of Jose Marins, at one time parish priest of 50,000 communicant Catholics in Brazil — 'The problem of how to cope with my parochial community just overwhelmed me. . . . The idea flashed into our minds: why don't we start from the people? Why don't we organise small groups? Let's go to them, let's push them to assume responsibility for their Christian community: we'll be the animators; pastoral action must be decentralised, so that lay people coordinate their communities and the priests assure the liaison between the communities and back up their leaders.'[18]

In what has been called 'the age of giantism', not least in the Christian church, we are being summoned again to discover that 'small is beautiful', not stunted; creative, not diminishing; releasing, not restricting. A tiny diamond is far more valuable than a lorryload of stones.

# CHAPTER 2

# Shoppers in the supermarket

*'A church in which everybody feels they are really somebody —
that is the way it ought to be; everyone with a name and a face. Yet
there are still people in the church who feel themselves to be
shoppers in the great supermarket of the faith.'*

Most of us probably know the experience of being strangers in a
large church, either as visitors or even as regular worshippers.
We want to get to know people, but it is too impersonal and the
opportunities never present themselves. Even when we became acquainted with one or two others, the conversation
tends to be stilted. We need a more relaxed and relaxing
atmosphere. Once in a more intimate group, it takes time,
effort and patience to build up good relationships. We also live
in a society, as Westerners, which is highly introspective and
self-critical about personal relationships: How am I coming
across? What are my real motives? Am I being honest and
open? Can I trust myself . . . or him/her? What am I getting
out of this relationship? Will I regret it? Will I have to suffer
pain or rejection?

## The model of Jesus

All the trends are, therefore, against the development of
trusting, open, self-giving, loving relationships between
Christians. The best place to start, as in everything, is with
the person and ministry of Jesus himself. One of the least
examined facets of his life is the way he modelled personal
relationships.[1] In order to appreciate how his example can
illumine personal relationships within the family of God,
especially in home churches, we need to take an overview of
all his relationships. This is best done by imagining them in
reverse order of concentration —

6. The crowds
5. Those who believed in Him
4. The 70
3. The 12
2. Peter, James & John
   Mary, Martha & Lazarus
1. John

## The crowds

Starting from the perimeter, it is instructive to see how Jesus related to crowds. We are told that, when he saw the crowds, 'he had compassion on them, because they were harassed and helpless, like sheep without a shepherd.'[2] He was constantly going out to them, giving himself to them in teaching, healing, deliverance and practical compassion. He did not shrink from such contact, but he did not major on it. At times he deliberately withdrew from it. This was not least to resource his personal relationship with his Father God, but it probably also reflects the limited importance he attached to such ministry.

## Those who believed

Amongst the crowds there were many who believed in Jesus and followed him. As the pace hotted up, substantial numbers fell by the wayside. This began to happen particularly as he steadfastly set his face to go to Jerusalem to certain violence and death, and not least when he refused to bow to their desire to make him king.[3] There seems to have been a particular crisis with such 'easy believers' when he began to talk about the need to eat his flesh and drink his blood. For Jewish sensitivities in particular this was rather too much to swallow and 'after this many turned back from following him.'

Yet in spite of these factors it is obviously true that there were significant numbers of people who not only believed in Jesus but stuck with him. These he taught. He gave them thorough teaching. He gave them comprehensive teaching. He gave them challenging teaching. He gave them teaching which refused to let them stand still in their faith and discipleship. If we take the comments of the synoptic evangel-ists about the nature of his teaching through parables, we conclude that the bulk of his teaching was given only to such disciples and not to the crowds. The parables were not simple stories about homely topics with spiritual truth radiating from them. They were 'weapons of warfare' which provoked his hearers into taking serious stock of their whole approach to life and to God and to eternity. If they chose to be serious about this, they joined the smaller group of 'disciples' who asked Jesus privately what these fascinating, but disturbing, stories were all about. In other words, the teaching of Jesus was very specifically and directly geared to those who wanted to move from simple titillation by an unusual guru to practical disci-pleship of a man who might even be God.

The fundamental importance of this perspective on the parables is dramatically underlined in the account, as well as the explanation, of the parable of the sower.[4] The key word throughout the 20 verses or so is 'hear'. In the Bible the word 'hear' has a full-blooded meaning, i.e. to hear, to take in, to understand, and to obey. Jesus says that the key to growing as a disciple is that kind of hearing applied to his teaching. By definition far more people were within earshot of his teaching than actually gave heed to it in obedience.

## The seventy

Now it was — and still is — with such people as the latter that Jesus is most concerned. It is from such 'disciples' of the real kind that he chooses out seventy to whom he entrusts part of his own apostolic commission.[5] Quite clearly he had another kind of relationship with these seventy. He sent them on ahead of him two by two into every town and place where he himself was about to come. He must have known them fairly well to give them such unattractive (to put it mildly) instruc-tions: 'Behold, I send you out as lambs in the midst of wolves. Carrry no purse, no bag, no sandals; and salute no one on the road.' He is clearly aware of a strong commitment on their part to him as Lord, because he is prepared to end their commission with these words 'he who hears you hears me, and he who rejects you rejects me, and he who rejects me rejects him who sent me.' It is difficult to imagine Jesus entrusting to an unknown group of stragglers, from amongst the vast crowds who followed him, such a radical commission. Precisely the same sense of close relationship comes through in the report-back by the seventy. Clearly their mission has been successful by any standard. They have seen things happening through their own ministry which previously they had seen only in the ministry of Jesus himself. He sees in them the permanent temptation to see success in Christian ministry as the criterion of approval by God. His comments are, in effect, underlining the primary value of a personal relationship with God through obedience to Jesus as Lord — 'do not rejoice in this (i.e. the authority I have given you over all the power of the enemy), but rejoice that your names are written in heaven.'

The very next words in the same chapter are very evocative of the distinctive relationship between Jesus and these seventy particular disciples. Having taught them to rejoice pre-eminently in their relationship with God as their Father, he himself then 'rejoiced in the Holy Spirit' and thanked the Father, 'Lord of Heaven and earth', that the eternal realities of life and death have been hidden from the intelligent and sophisticated, but are now being revealed only to those whom he, Jesus, chooses to inform about them. These people he actually calls 'babes'.

## The disciples

On the other hand these seventy were a distinct group from those who are, in the normal narrative of the synoptic gospels, called the disciples. These are regarded as of such importance that they are called by name. Before Jesus actually chose them, he went up into the hills and spent a night praying, presumably to become attuned to his Father's choice for such an important group of people.[6] Subsequent events and informed interpretation alike show us that they were a very mixed bunch of people. Politically they had within them a quisling in the form of Matthew the tax-collector. Yet cheek by jowl with Matthew was Simon Zelotes — the Zealot — who was so far from being a friend of the Romans that they would have called him a terrorist and would have been after his blood. Fellow-Jews would have called him a freedom fighter. Matthew and Simon had as much in common as Ian Paisley and the Pope.

There were also obvious differences in temperament — John the mystic, together with the sons of Zebedee who were so tempestuous that they were nicknamed 'Sons of Thunder'. It is difficult to imagine how the impetuous temper of Peter could possibly have lived side by side with the pessimistic skepticism of Thomas. And how they all coped with the greed of Judas, together with his eventual betrayal, only Jesus himself could tell us.

In spite of everything, these twelve men were bound together in such a tight community that they spent virtually the whole of every day for three full years in one another's pockets. And in that time Jesus did not let them get away with anything. Time and time again he rammed home the same lessons. He taught them by example, he taught them by repetition; he taught them by their mistakes; he taught them by observation, he taught them in prayer, he taught them in reproof; he taught them in pairs, he taught them as individuals, he taught them as a group. He gave himself to them all the way across the board and there was nothing about him which they did not observe. If they missed a trick, it was because they were not men of observation.

But the most important thing that we can say about the relationship between Jesus and these twelve men was that he loved them. John says, when talking about one of the most poignant and dramatic moments in the whole of their life together, 'having loved his own who were in the world, he loved them to the end.'[7] Another version says that he was about to show them the full extent of his love. How did he do that? This is where we need to take a very close look at the context of both those remarks and the actions which surround them. This is the passage where Jesus gave these twelve disciples what he called 'a new commandment'. This was very simple — 'love one another as I have loved you'. We need to say straightaway that he did not give that new commandment to the crowds who followed him in such large numbers, or to the considerable multitude of people who had some measure of faith in him, or even to the seventy whom he commissioned with some special ministry. This commandment was given to a group of men with whom he had spent his whole life for three full years and from whom he had concealed nothing. He had laid down his life for them in all kinds of metaphorical ways and he was now about to lay down his life for them literally.

This commandment is given in the context of the Last Supper, a special part of a meal in an upper room in a secret house somewhere in the beleaguered town of Jerusalem — beleaguered because the authorities were out for his blood. It was dangerous to be with Jesus and nobody else knew where they were. That is why there were no domestic servants to do the normal chores, one of which was to wash the feet of the guests, who had walked on sandalled feet through the dusty streets to reach their venue. All the way through the meal it might have crossed the minds of every disciple as to who should do that domestic chore. Not one of them chose to do it. So they had agreed silently that it should not be done. But Jesus would not let it pass. 'After supper, he girded himself with a towel and washed the disciples' feet.' At least Simon Peter had the grace to object that this was the last thing which he, Jesus, should do to them. What Peter did not appreciate was that this was the entire basis for the relationship between Jesus and these twelve disciples. It was a relationship of service by the greater of the lesser: 'If I then, your Lord and Master, wash your feet, you also ought to wash one another's feet.' This is the basis of this unique relationship between Jesus and the twelve. It is arguable that this statement, which enunciated what it means to be within the close company of the friends of Jesus, was the final straw which broke the back of Judas's continued attempts to make Jesus the person to liberate the Jews from Roman oppression.

Yet, the love of Jesus for those twelve, including, Judas, is such that he does not, even then, jettison the man who will betray him. He uses a particular social convention, offering a piece of bread dipped in wine, to give the betrayer one more chance to accept his love and friendship. Judas rejects it, leaves the meal table, leaves the room leaves the house, leaves the possibility of eternal life — 'and it was night.'

All that we have been saying underlines the remarkable distinctiveness of the relationship between Jesus and these twelve men. Actually the commandment to love one another in the same way as he loves them is given after the removal of Judas. Judas would have been unable to contemplate applying himself to such a commandment. The other eleven found it difficult enough. In essence the love of Jesus for those men was totally unconditional and this he demonstrated in the next 24 hours. We must do nothing to minimize the fact that it is this kind of love which marks out Christians. If there is not such love amongst Christians, then we will not know that we belong to Jesus, nor will the world believe that Jesus is the One sent by God to be the Saviour of the world.[8] Therefore the most significant issues in the universe depend upon the reality of the love which Christians have for one another.

## The three

Having said this about the relationship between Jesus and the twelve, we still have to notice that there were certain occasions during those three years when Jesus demonstrated a special relationship with three of the twelve — Peter, James, and John. He allowed them access to experiences which were denied to the other nine, e.g. on the mountain of the Transfiguration and in the garden of Gethsemane.[9] It seems pointless to ask why Jesus should have chosen these three, rather than any of the other nine. That seems to have been his privilege. Of course, all three were due to have up-front ministries in the life of the apostolic church, but the relationship he offered to them during those three years before his death hardly met with the kind of response which would have made him likely to entrust them with greater responsibility. In other words, the way Jesus relates to those three in love is as unconditional as the way he related to the twelve, or to the seventy, or to the multitudes who believed in him, or even to the vast crowds with whom he came into frequent contact.

Clearly Jesus also had a distinctive relationship with Lazarus, Mary and Martha. He used their home in Bethany as a place to escape, unwind and be refreshed. They ministered to his needs, and by his presence he brought great blessing to them — both in crisis and in the routine.[9a]

When we ask ourselves what is the nature of such love, we almost are bound to ignore patterns of friendship which are normal in human relationships. Jesus himself gives us one of the most eloquent expositions of this love, this friendship.[10] He describes love as shown in no greater way than when 'a man lays down his life for his friends.' We all say 'Amen' to that. But Jesus continues: 'You are my friends if you do what I command you. No longer do I call you servants (or slaves) for the servant (slave) does not know what his master is doing; but I have called you friends, for all that I have heard from my Father I have made known to you.'

If, then, we want to understand the nature of the friendship Jesus revealed, we have to emphasise that it is one which lays down its life; it is one which is rooted in obedience to his commandments; it is one which is based on increasing knowledge of all that our Father God wants us to do and to be. That is true friendship and that is the friendship to which we are all called as disciples of Jesus. Jesus chose to make us his friends. We did not choose to make him our friend. He chose us with a purpose, and the purpose is that we should live lives that have eternal significance and effectiveness. It is our relationship with the Father sustained and deepened in prayer, which determines the quality of that friendship. So Jesus ends this passage with the repeated words, 'This I command you, to love one another.'

## The beloved disciple

Now there still is one further relationship in the earthly life of Jesus which we have not yet touched, and that is the distinctive (though not necessarily exclusive) friendship which he had with John 'the beloved disciple'. There was clearly, a very distinctive quality of sharing between the two, as is indicated by John's position next to the breast of Jesus while they were reclining at table during the Last Supper. It is probably true to say that the highly distinctive nature of John's gospel can be attributed mainly to the peculiar intimacy which he enjoyed with Jesus. Certainly John penetrated something of the depths of the nature of Jesus as God/man in ways which seem to have been only glimpsed by others who walked and talked with him. Having said this, there seems no warrant for believing that the ground for Jesus' relationship with John was any different from the ground of his relationship with the others.

It is important to stress that we are not talking about different *levels* of relationship in the life of Jesus, so much as different *kinds* of relationship. It would be misleading to say that Jesus had a *deeper* relationship with John that with James and Peter; or that those three had a *deeper* relationship with Jesus than the other nine. What matters to us today is to discover the ways in which we can have the kind of relationships which Jesus modelled for us in his earthly life. If he is the perfect man and if our true humanity is to be discovered in allowing his Spirit to control our daily lives, then we can expect the Spirit of Jesus to lead us into similar relationships. We have taken some time examining the nature of Jesus' relationships — to the 'beloved disciple', John; to John, James and Peter; to the family at Bethany; to the twelve apostles; to the seventy commissioned missionaries; to the large numbers of disciples who believed in him; and to the vast multitude who thronged him. This pattern was possible only because of the centrifugal nature of his relationship with his heavenly Father.

## Complete sharing

It is a moot point whether Jesus needed either to examine that relationship with God in any high-powered way, or even whether he experienced any compulsion to examine the inner dynamics of any of his interpersonal relationships. He shares himself completely with those whom he called his friends, in precisely the same way as his Heavenly Father shares himself completely with him. The result was that he could make the astonishing claim 'all that the Father has I have declared to you.' That is the basis, the only basis, of true friendship. If we have to work out whether we can afford that or whether the cost of such sharing is too great, then our experience of friendship is less than Christian.

At this point, it is crucial to stress that the gift of the Spirit after Pentecost makes such friendship pre-eminently possible. Indeed without such a gift it is not possible. This presumably is why Jesus gave 'the new commandment' in the first place, not in order to hold a 'sword of Damocles' over our heads, but because he knew that such a way of life is actually possible in the power of the same Spirit who controlled his own life.

We can see the truth of this by returning to the original nature of the relationship which Jesus had with the crowds. Often we read that they could not themselves take the cost of such close relating to Jesus as Lord. They had too much to lose and they knew it. They were in the relationship for what they could get out of it. Their relationship was not one of sharing but of taking. They wanted their needs met, their diseases healed, their problems solved, their aspirations fulfilled. They did not want the full implications of friendship with God. They had their personal and their political agendas. They had their family and their business loyalties. For many of them the problem was that their daily work was more important than the quality of their relationship with the God/man.

### The cost of true friendship

There were, also, those who had so many vested interests that they had no intention whatsoever of entering into any relationship with Jesus. These are epitomised by those who held religious and therefore political power in the land. Those who wield most power, find it most difficult to enter into true friendship with Jesus. It is the very nature of Jesus which makes such friendship costly for those with status and position. It is not coincidence that the common people heard him gladly. They were glad because, unlike people such as the scribes and Pharisees, there was nothing for them to lose — or very little. Indeed one of the most obvious — and most frequently noted — characteristics of the way Jesus related to people is that he had an irresistible attraction for those who were drummed out of normal society — e.g. lepers, prostitutes, tax-collectors, Samaritans, and others who were for various reasons unclean or unacceptable. He also made it plain that the friendship he offered was on his own terms, however unconditional they were. He said, 'Follow me.' He was pepared to call people to hand over everything, to cut all their previous ties in order to make friendship with him paramount. At times he made it plain that such friendship was impossible unless these ties were terminated.

The essential nature of this relationship is beautifully summed up in Mark's record of Jesus choosing his original twelve: 'He appointed them to be with him and to be sent out to preach and have authority to cast out demons.'[11] In other words, friendship with Jesus is first being with him, before it is ever being sent out to do his work. Mark also says that he called to him 'those whom he desired', presumably the result of having become attuned through a night of prayer with the mind and heart of God.

It could never be said of Jesus that he totally ignored his mother and his brothers. At the same time, there were two or three occasions when he made it abundantly plain that God's purpose, planning, and pleasure were infinitely more important to him than the demands of those linked with him by natural kinship.[12] In brief, therefore, friendship with Jesus demands total commitment to him as Lord. It introduces us into the reality of a friendship which plumbs the very secrets of God himself. It is a reality which grows when we spend more time together, not as we examine its inner dynamics. It is based on uniting factors which transcend all the normal differences which keep people apart. It therefore can bind in a common loyalty people of totally different backgrounds and convictions. It is a friendship with a definite and a divine purpose, namely that we should bear fruit in all kinds of active service and transparent goodness. In other words, it is not to be enjoyed for its own sake, nor is it to be indulged in as a personal luxury. It is for giving away, not for grasping. And its own prototype is the relationship between Jesus and his Father which is superbly described by Paul: 'Have this mind among yourselves which you have in Christ Jesus who, though he was in the form of God, did not account equality with God a thing to be grasped, but emptied himself, taking the form of a servant, being born in the likeness of men. And being found in human form he humbled himself and became obedient unto death, even death on a cross.'[13]

## John Wesley's pattern

This pattern of personal relationships, modelled for us by Jesus, should become our inspiration for relating to one another as brothers and sisters, particularly in home churches. The community ethics of the New Testament are grounded in this divine pattern. One of the most successful and well-known examples of such church life is the work of John Wesley, who drafted all those who responded to his preaching into 'classes'. One of Wesley's men, Henry Fish, who later wrote a manual for class leaders, put it like this:

'It is as clear as daylight that that kind of communion (i.e. experienced in class meetings) has the express warrant of Holy Scripture; and that something more than church communion in the sacrament of the Lord's Supper was enjoyed by the primitive Christians. They had 'fellowship' as well as 'breaking of bread'. How, for instance, could they exhort one another daily? How could they comfort and edify one another? How could they provoke one another to love and good works? How could they confess their faults to one another, and pray for one another? How teach and admonish one another in psalms and hymns and spiritual songs? How bear one another's burdens? How weep with those who weep, and rejoice with those who rejoice, if they never meet together for the purpose of conversing on experimental religion, and the state of each other's souls? Whatever persons may say to the contrary, those churches, the members of which do not observe, or in which they have not the opportunity of observing, the foregoing precepts which are enjoined in the New Testament Scriptures, are not based on the model of the apostolic churches.'[14]

Apart from his unique preaching and evangelistic ministry, John Wesley had remarkable organising ability. He applied this thoroughly to the three-fold structure which soon emerged in the wake of his preaching up and down the country. Every person who responded was enrolled in a *class*, under the pastoral oversight of the class leader. Wesley was increasingly concerned that new believers often 'grew cold and gave way to the sins which had long easily beset them.' By 1742 in Bristol (i.e. four years after his Aldersgate Street experience of assurance of salvation through trusting Christ), there were 1,100 people divided into classes of 12 each, each with a leader whose responsibility it was 'to make a particular inquiry into the behaviour of those he saw weekly.'[15] Class members began to 'bear one another's burdens' and naturally to 'care for one another.' Wesley saw the class meetings as the disciplinary unit. All accepted members of the classes together constituted the *society* in that place, which met quarterly for the eucharist. The third group was the *band*, a smaller group of either men or women, averaging about half a dozen, who met at least once a week with the express purpose of fulfilling the biblical injunction 'Confess your faults one to another, and pray for one another, that you may be healed.'[16] It has been estimated that about 20 percent of class members met also in these bands. At each meeting of the bands, four questions were asked of each person present:

'(i) What known sins have you committed since our last meeting?

(ii) What temptations have you met with?

(iii) How were you delivered?

(iv) What have you thought, said or done, of which you doubt whether it be sin or not?'[17]

Obviously, there was an intimacy in the bands which was not seen to be appropriate at the class meeting. There was no chosen leader in the bands, whereas the class leader was crucial for pastoral oversight and discipline.

'Wesley's gift for organisation was bent towards the one objective of forming a genuine people of God within the institutional chuch. . . . The secret of his radicality lay in his forming little groups of God-seekers who joined together in an earnest quest to be Jesus' disciples. Wesley would have nothing of solitary religion, secret Christians, or faith without works.'[18]

How does Wesley's pattern of society, class and band fit in with the example we have seen in Jesus' personal rela-, tionships? It can readily be seen that, structurally at least these three correspond (closely, if not completely) to Jesus' relationships with Peter, James and John; the twelve apostles; and the seventy (or perhaps the wider group of disciples in any one place). Of course, no structure can begin to guarantee Christlike relationships, only the love of God shed abroad in our hearts by the Holy Spirit can do that. There is evidence that such love did mark the community-life of the people who came to be called 'methodists' When the love began to be lost, the pattern also began to disappear.

Wesley himself was under no illusion about the way the pattern he established followed closely the model of the New Testament: 'It can scarce be conceived what advantages have been reaped from this little prudential regulation. Many now happily experienced that Christian fellowship of which they had not so much an idea before. They began to 'bear one another's burdens', and naturally to 'care for each other'. As they had daily a more intimate acquaintance with, so they had a more endeared affection for, each other. And 'speaking the truth in love, they grew up into Him in all things, who is the Head, even Christ'.'[19]

'A church in which everybody feels they are really some-body — that is the way it ought to be': not shoppers in the great supermarket, but valued and appreciated members of the family, reflecting the love of Jesus across the whole range of personal relationships.

# CHAPTER 3

# An uprooted plant

*'Every community which goes to make up the church of a particular place, whether it be of a city, a district or a household, ought to put down roots in that place. A rootless church is like an uprooted plant: it will soon wither away.'*

Part of the price we pay for motor cars is a commuter attitude to church membership. In most urban areas in the West, there is a multitude of choices for Christians or would-be worshippers. If one church is unacceptable for any reason whatever, you hop in your car and find one you like. In many areas of the U.S.A., particularly California, it is not unusual to belong to a church 30, 40 or even 50 miles from your home. This 'freeway fellowship' hits right at the heart of what it is to be the church, to be the salt and the light in a given community.

Even community churches can become so introverted that they never actually influence their locality with the gospel. The faithful gather at the shrine week by week; some may meet in different homes for Bible study and prayer. But the net impact on the community is minimal. In most middle-class localities a major reason for this ineffectiveness is the lack of any distinctiveness in daily living. The lifestyle of Christians differs from that of non-believers in a few outward actions only. A few obvious excesses are avoided, but there is not much that is salty or incandescent about such a church.

## Christian sub-culture

Paradoxically, while adopting a very similar lifestyle in material ways, such Christians actually develop a sub-culture which excludes non-Christians from any normal or natural encounter with Christians. Innumerable church meetings, friendships which are almost exclusively within the Christian group, absence from the natural meeting-points of the community, uneasiness in mixing with unbelievers — these and other factors all amount to a lifestyle which, though superficially very similar to that of unbelievers, is actually far removed from them.

Unfortunately, it seems unlikely that the motor car will disappear or that people will stop choosing which church they want to attend. If, however, home churches are encouraged to take root wherever Christians live, there is a hope that once again the witness of the church will take root as a corporate reality. Indeed, there is no reason why such microcosms of the church should not emerge where Christians work and play, as well as where they live: the realities of modern living mean that most Christians have three such arenas. It may well be that Christians in a work situation or a leisure activity will meet in mutual support rather than as a home church. In that case, they will share the dynamics of Wesley's small bands, rather than the larger classes. There is certainly an urgent need for Christians in different settings and occupations to work out together what it means to be disciples of Jesus right there.

The point of substance is this: wherever Christians gather together, they must send down roots in that place. If this does not happen, there is no context for their discipleship, no relevance or even opportunity for bearing witness to Jesus as Lord, no authentic demonstration of the life and message of the church. It is of the essence of home churches, therefore, that they become rooted in the community where they meet. Specific ways in which this can be done will become apparent on subsequent pages. For the present let us consider a number of examples to whet our appetites. Not all of these will strictly illustrate the home church sending down roots in the local community, but each illustrates what it means to be committed to the locality where God has placed us.

Many of the features of the Christian community-life described in Acts 2 were deliberately repeated into the later monasteries, which at their best were designed to be working models of the kingdom of heaven. 'Their walls could not hide the piety and the industry . . . and many of them became civilizing influences on the surrounding towns, exerting a positive influence on their spiritual, economic and social life.'[1]

## Wesley's roots

John Wesley's pattern of church life clearly rooted Christians where they lived. It is quite likely that the inspiration for this pattern began in his childhood home at Epworth, where his father, Samuel, was the Rector. Samuel Wesley was keen on the Anglican societies which sprang up in the early eighteenth century in different parts of England. These societies combined a deep spirituality with practical involvement in social need amongst the poor and disadvantaged. Samuel saw in them the opportunity of reviving the good elements of the long-discredited monastic movement, 'without many of the inconveniences of it.'[1a]

What John Wesley's father hankered after, his mother, Susanna, began to put into practice — and that in a way that rather scared the cautious Samuel. When he was away on a protracted visit to London in 1712, Susanna began a small meeting in the parsonage at Epworth on Sunday evenings. It grew out of the devotional time she spent with her family — at the time John was nine, Charles four. A few neighbours asked to join, followed by several others in the village. The group grew fairly swiftly from 30 to 200. Susanna would read a sermon, pray and talk with those who came. It dramatically increased the numbers attending regular services in the church, caused great jealousy in the clergyman standing in for Samuel, and eventually aroused her husband's anxiety, fears and ultimate censorship. Samuel, like so many clergymen, liked the theory, but found the practice of such local grassroots discipleship too threatening to his reputation, office and comforts.[2]

We can only guess at the impact this experiment in vital Christian community-life made on the young John Wesley. Clearly, his mother's character, ability, spirituality, initiative and sheer strength of will must have rubbed off on her son. She came to the Church of England out of a nonconformist background and was obviously a woman of independent spirit and great enterprise. The year 1712 showed John Wesley what could be done by sending down roots into the local community, using a Christian home as a base of operations. The classes he later established 'were in effect house churches (not classes for instruction, as the term 'class' might suggest), meeting in the various neighbourhoods where people lived. The class leaders (men and women) were pastors and disciplers.'[3] It has been estimated that by 1798 the numbers of 'methodists' in Wesley's classes (he himself died in 1791) was 101,712. 'By the turn of the century one in every thirty adult Englishmen were methodists.'[4] By sending down roots in every place, these home churches were growing so strong and healthy that we can appreciate the grounds for the oft-quoted (though hotly-disputed) remark, that England was saved from a bloody revolution, such as engulfed France, by the impact of Wesley's life.

## Wesley in London

His commitment to local, grassroots Christian community is most clearly seen in the growth of his headquarters at the Foundry in Moorfields in London's East End. He gradually turned it into a community centre for the area. As well as holding two weekly prayer-meetings, a daily preaching service at 5 a.m., and as many as 66 class-meetings a week, the reclaimed cannon foundry eventually housed the first free dispensary in London since the dissolution of the monasteries two hundred years previously. Wesley's initiative brought about a free school for sixty local children and a shelter for widows in the same building. There were meals provided for the poor, with whom Wesley used to eat when he was in London — he had a set of rooms on the second floor of the Foundry. There was also a bookshop which sold volumes of his sermons.[5] Wesley's expression of Christian community-life in the heart of the city of London has been likened to Augustine's ministry at Hippo in the 6th century. He surrounded himself with helpers, priests and parishioners in his desire to reflect 'the city of God' in the neighbourhood.

## Wilberforce

Another famous name in English history is William Wilberforce, who died three days after the House of Commons passed the third reading of his bill for the abolition of slavery on July 26, 1833.[6] Wilberforce was one of the 'Clapham sect', a small group of Christian men in different careers who met regularly in the parish of Clapham under the care of the Rector, John Venn, for mutual encouragement, prayer and Bible study. John Newton, by this time a respected clergyman in the city of London but formerly the captain of ships devoted to carrying slaves from Africa to the New World, also provided spiritual counsel to Wilberforce in his labours to abolish slavery. This small band of brothers were responsible for founding both the Church Missionary Society in 1799 ('for missions to Africa and the East' — Newton was also involved) and the British and Foreign Bible Society in 1804. The Bible Society came into being in response to the story of a young Welsh girl from Bala, who trekked across the mountains to find a Bible: this led the 'Clapham sect' to ask, 'If for Wales, why not for the whole world?'

Wilberforce's Clapham home, Broomfield, gradually became the focus of strong Christian witness in the neighbourhood. 'The Wilberforces kept 13 or 14 servants outside and inside the house, which was about normal for their rank in life. But Wilberforce tended to enlist domestics who were deserving rather than efficient, nor would he cast off the useless or infirm until they found suitable berths. . . . Servants adored William, who would sit beside them when they were ill and turn a blind eye to their shortcomings on duty. . . . The whole house attended family prayers twice daily.' Thus, Broomfield provided a secure base for Wilberforce himself, and for many others in Clapham or who visited the home. 'Clapham neighbours and their children were in and out. . . . There were other children in the circle — black boys, sons of Sierra Leone chiefs whom Zachary Macaulay (the governor and a Christian) had brought home for education as leaders and missionaries among their own peoples. . . . No differences of race or colour interfered. . . . Clapham pioneered racial equality.' Apparently, Wilberforce had a great love for and enjoyment in all children — yet another mark of the man's rounded Christian witness. His small band of brothers and his extended family lifestyle both alike brought him into close

contact with the communities in which he either worked or
lived.'

## Local involvement

Moving into the experiences and example of today's church,
the life of the Latin American grassroots communities teems
with pointers to such local involvement. In Nicaragua in 1980,
the nation's secondary-school and university students were
mobilised for a highly-successful literacy crusade. The grassroots communities, especially in the rural areas, were a
crucial factor in this crusade, which reduced illiteracy from
50% to 20% in a matter of months. They played this
significant role precisely because 'they were already the
natural point of contact for reaching the people most in
need.'[7] If home churches make a priority of sending down
roots deep into their neighbourhood, sooner or later they will
each become significant agents of 'shalom'. The experience in
Portezuelo described in the last chapter amply illustrates that.

A further example comes from Vitoria: 'in one remote
location, the people demanded a bus service to get them to
work, but the transport company alleged that the road was too
narrow. The people measured the width of the road and
proved them wrong, and obliged the company to act. Another
grassroots community built a health centre. In each case
scheming politicians moved in, trying to claim the credit when
the work was done — to the derision of the people.'[8]

The grassroots communities are formed on the basis of
geographical proximity. From an initial awareness of personal
problems, members go on to discover those of the family, of
the neighbourhood, the district, the town, the country. Unless
there is some significant degree of physical closeness, it is hard
to envisage any home church truly putting down roots outside
itself. Communities like those in Nicaragua, Portezuelo and
Vitoria inevitably are part and parcel of their local situation,
simply because the people in them are who they are —
'industrial workers, agricultural workers, landless peasants,
small farmers that do not own the land, shepherds, part-time
workers, the unemployed, displaced persons, servants,
washerwomen, manual labourers, prostitutes, delinquent or

abandoned young people, the illiterate, migrants, the mentally and physically handicapped, beggars, old people who are all alone in the world.'[9] Such people have nowhere to go to hide from the realities of their situation. When they comprise a grassroots community, they have already been firmly grounded in the life of that neighbourhood.

## Individualism

Private property, and other privacies which money can buy, enable many Christians to live in little boxes, insulated from their neighbours and their community. It is essential that such Christians discover a corporate lifestyle which breaks out of this isolation into the needs and pains of others who are trapped in their own little boxes. We can take our inspiration from members of the grassroots communities: these people 'leave individualism behind and commit themselves as a group, because their life or their very survival is at stake. The grassroots community focuses the interests of the people, so that a collective commitment becomes possible.'[10]

## Asian pointers

We started this chapter on the theme of today's high mobility. We will end with observations in the same vein from two Asian countries. In Singapore the same problem faces the churches, in spite of its greatly-restricted land area. Most churches apparently have a mixture of those living nearby and those travelling some distance. 'In these circumstances we have to differentiate between 'catchment area' and 'community of responsibility'. The first is primarily a territorial concept, referring to the area immediately around the church; the second is a people concept, allowing a congregation to target on a certain group or groups of people . . . with whom church members already have some fruitful contact. . . . It would appear odd, for example, if a church containing a large number of commuters was very church-building centred in its activities. Should it not decentralise? . . . In land-tight Singapore, it would appear that many Christians are very sanctuary- or meeting place-centred rather than locality-centred in their thinking.'[11]

The genius of the Full Gospel Central Church in Seoul lies in its head-on tackling of the need to decentralise by its network of home cell units throughout the city. The church's pastor, Paul Yonggi Cho, speaks realistically of the continuous threat of communist invasion, from which Korea was rescued less than thirty years ago: 'If the communists came into Seoul, they would kill me and probably murder all the pastors. They could demolish the church buildings, but they could never destroy the church.' Why? Because the home cell system is so meshed into the very fabric of society, that it can resist even the most persistent pursuers. The home cells are spread throughout the city, and it would be impossible for any invader fully to discover and destroy them. The organisation is so large that no one person knows where all the cells are, and instructions have been given that every record must be immediately destroyed in the event of invasion.[12] It is difficult to conceive of a situation where the church has roots more securely planted in the community than that.

CHAPTER 4

# The very best sprinkling-machine

*'You can buy and plant the best sort of seeds, and purchase the very best sprinkling-machine. But if the seeds aren't watered every day, and if the sun doesn't shine, then plants are going to die. . . . The church may be all very fine and well-organised, but if it lacks the water which is the faith of the people, and the sun which is the Spirit of God, it grows weak. . . .'*

'The letter kills, but the Spirit gives life'[1] is as true of church structures as of the two covenants of law and grace. No amount of good organisation by John Wesley was able to bring life to the people of 18th century England. The home cell units in Seoul are not the causes but the channels of growth. Equally, the grassroots communities of Latin America 'enjoy the liberty and creativity of groups of human beings who are sensitive to the unpredictable breath of the Spirit. They really are a church which is born of the people by the power of the Spirit.'[2]

These two realities, the lifegiving work of the Spirit and the spontaneous motivation of ordinary Christians, contain the secret of moving in the stream of God's purposes. Time and time again those in church leadership positions find themselves either too wary or too manipulative to follow the wind of the Spirit. We see all the potential risks of letting the people be the church and we put on the brakes, for fear of the vehicle careering out of control. Alternatively, we are fired by a vision of what the church can become and is called to be; but, instead of praying and loving people into choosing that path, we stampede them prematurely and reluctantly into a pattern for which they are not ready and about which they have no inner conviction. It requires wisdom from above to detect the authentic signs of the Spirit's own movement, so that we can move in alongside and cooperate with him in his work of bringing life in renewal.

## Not overnight

In applying this to the matter of home churches, it is important to remind ourselves of a simple, but basic, fact: it is most unlikely that these will emerge overnight as the God-given pattern for a congregation. In most cases it will be a question of gradually moving existing small groups a few steps forward towards the reality of being home churches. This was the case with the grassroots communities.

'They are not like Melchizedek, without father or mother. They do not arise in history as if they had descended from heaven, without human intervention. They have their social and ecclesiastical context. There they germinated, absorbed the goodness of the soil, and emerged into the light.'[3]

It will be valuable to note the signs of spiritual renewal which preceded and gave rise to the grassroots communities in Brazil.[4] The Holy Spirit works with distinctive newness in each age and each situation, but these signs may well have their parallels in our own context.

## Tracing spiritual history

The first sign was the strong involvement of the laity in the Brazilian church before the middle of the 19th century. During the next 100 years the dominant, if not oppressive, influence of Rome was throttling the life of the church. Only in the last 20 years has this stranglehold been released, allowing the grassroots communities to flourish. Before 1850, the figure of the layman was central. This showed itself above all through flourishing church institutions, such as the fraternities, brotherhoods and third orders. Their direction was in the hands of the laity. They were separate and autonomous entities. Two notable characteristics of this lay movement were a strong emphasis on family devotions (which were marked by great warmth of spirit) and an exuberant enjoyment of religious celebration at great festivals (the *fiesta* phenomenon of the Latin).[3a]

It may seem extravagant to trace our spiritual heritage back into the dim and distant past, but it seems increasingly possible that areas, cities and countries have a spiritual *ambiance* which is significantly created by what has happened a long time ago in that place. The study of church history is not simply for the specialist, nor is it merely a subject which has its own fascination. Pursued carefully and sensitively, it can provide clues both to the way God wants to work today, and to the reasons why there is resistance to the Spirit in a given place at a given time.

For example, in the 1870's in South Africa the wind of the Spirit began to blow strongly in a certain section of the Dutch Reformed church in Wellington, Cape Province. The local pastor was Andrew Murray. Ordinary folk in his congregation were visited by the Spirit and began to gather informally in the church hall for prayer and praise. On two successive nights Andrew Murray tried to call a halt to the proceedings. He then recognized the authentic work of God, and the Lord used his preaching ministry to bring renewal into many parts of the D.R.C. Eventually, the church hierarchy took fright and stamped on it, restoring the life of that denomination to the stern, unbending authoritarianism which has so undergirded the system of *apartheid*. During the last five years or so, there have been signs of fresh renewal in the D.R.C. It remains to be seen whether its leaders will be able to encourage this spiritual life, or at least give it room to grow, instead of stamping it out once more. Whatever happens, the seeds of new life are in the soil.

## Oxford — a case in point

The situation in Oxford is another interesting case in point. At the head of St. Giles stands the Martyrs' Memorial, erected in the heyday of the Tractarian revival in the middle of the 19th century to recall the death by burning of Cranmer, Ridley and Latimer in 1555–6. Cranmer's words to Ridley, as they faced death together, still ring eloquent chords in any called to minister the gospel in Oxford today. 'Be of good comfort, Master Ridley, we shall this day light a candle by God's grace in England as, I trust, shall never be put out.' By the 1830's, the Evangelical Revival focused in the Wesleys and George Whitefield had begun to flatten out and become respectable. The time was ripe for another movement which would enrich aspects of Christianity which the revival of evangelical life had not touched, especially dignity and awe in worship. Inevitably, this Oxford Movement (spearheaded by John Keble, John Henry Newman and Edward Pusey) 'cherished the Catholic heritage of the church rather than the Protestant changes'[5] brought about at the Reformation. That is why the Martyrs' Memorial was erected at this time, as a further protest against what was perceived by evangelicals as a threatened return to the errors of unreformed catholicism. Today in Oxford one of the keys to a spiritual breakthrough could well be a similar courage in holding firm to 'the truth as it is in Jesus',[6] in an intellectual climate which prizes the ability to speak cleverly and articulately instead of the knowledge of truth. This defence and proclamation of the truth of the gospel needs to be rooted in an experience of worshipping God 'in spirit and in truth.'[7] Spiritual renewal in Oxford, if we learn the lessons of our history, will therefore be a response to 'the Spirit of truth . . . who will guide you into all the truth.'[8]

## Trusting the laity

If the first pointer to renewal by the Spirit in the Brazilian church was its early history of lay involvement, the second sign could be seen in the way laymen were entrusted with pastoral responsibility in Barra do Pirai in North East Brazil in 1956. This step was forced upon the Catholic church by a shortage of priests — an expedient which has often sparked new life. Apparently, during a pastoral visitation, the bishop, Angelo Rossi, was told by an old woman: 'In Natal the three Protestant churches are lit up and crowded. We hear their hymn-singing . . . and our Catholic church, closed, is in darkness . . . because we don't get a priest.'[9] The bishop was stung into mobilising 372 community coordinators, who gathered the people to pray, to listen to the reading of Scripture, to hold mass without a priest and in other ways to maintain a sense of community.

## Proclaiming the Gospel

At about the same time, the diocese of Natal pioneered a full-blooded programme of 'education for change' amongst the desperately needy people of the area. As well as an extensive literacy programme and education in health and agricultural skills, there was also a determined attempt at evangelisation, 'to take God to neglected communities.' Using local radio, the church had established a network of grassroots communities around numerous 'radio schools'. By 1963 there were 1,410 of these schools in the archdiocese of Natal alone. This movement is seen as a forerunner laying the ground for more mature grassroots communities.

## Breaking the mould

The fourth sign of emerging spiritual life took place not far from Natal in the small country-town of Nizia Floresta. Here a community of nuns, involved in pastoral care in that area, were moved by the Spirit to establish communities of prayer, working and life among the people. As a result of their experience, those in religious orders in other places were provoked into making big changes in their whole approach to their calling. They began to move out far more freely into pastoral enabling and support of the laity. Previous watertight conceptions of ministry were blown wide open — always a necessary preparation for and element in any home church pattern.

## Winning the hierarchy

The fifth sign of new life was when the hierarchy of the church began to identify more and more strongly with the ordinary people, particularly when, from 1964, Brazil entered a period of heavily oppressive and repressive military government — from which it still suffers. Significant groups of people with power in the church went to be with the poor. The more the working classes felt the pressure of government action, the more the church officially allied itself with them. A concerted effort was made to educate church leaders about the harsh realities of the situation — 18,000 courses for bishops and clergy were held up and down the country in five years. The laity were gradually becoming fully involved in the life of the church. The liturgical side of worship also underwent a transformation, in order to accommodate greater lay participation and the urge for more personal involvement in worship. Clergy, nuns and other full-time religious workers were steadily redeployed in order to strengthen the church's witness amongst the poor and the oppressed. Thus, the way was paved for the emergence of full-blown grassroots communities as a new way of being the church.

Let us pause to re-emphasize these five pointers or signs of the Holy Spirit at work in the church in Brazil *before* the grassroots communities were truly established — strong lay involvement way back in the early 19th century; lay ministry in the 1950's when there was a shortage of priests; direct evangelisation at the same period, hand-in-hand with meeting basic educational needs; 'professional' ministers (in this case, nuns) being released by the Spirit to pursue new patterns of worship and fellowship; and a gradual process of educating those in leadership in the church, to the point where they began to give whole-hearted support to the grassroots. Any or all of these signs are likely to have their parallels in every situation where the Holy Spirit is at work.

There are many indications today that members of the Latin American grassroots communities are discovering this essential encounter between genuine faith and the vibrancy of the Holy Spirit. The way Christians actually perceive their experiences of being the church is as good a pointer as any to its spiritual vitality. Consider this assessment of grassroots communities, drawn from the reports made by members at a number of regional conferences:

(i) 'There is the consciousness of being called *ekkletoi*, an essential experience of being the church. . . .'

(ii) This ecclesial awareness 'is intrinsically linked to being the people, concerned about one another's material and spiritual problems'. This is the true meaning of 'community'.

(iii) The participatory dimension is the characteristic that distinguishes the grassroots communities from the old church. In the words of one participant, 'Today the church belongs to everybody; all are owners of the church.'

(iv) The new ecclesial community now perceives that the priest 'is not a superior being but rather, a friend.' In the new church 'everyone has the rights that the priest had (including the distribution of the bread at the eucharist); all together are responsible for the church.'

(v) The grassroots communities have discovered the long-dormant biblical dimension. 'The Bible is no longer the book of the Protestants; it is accessible to all the people.' One participant commented: 'Earlier, if one went about with the Bible under one's arm, the person would be ridiculed; now the Bible has become part of the household and has even helped to overcome divisions amongst believers. Now, since we have begun to learn how to read the Bible, we find it speaks to our daily life; it has been popularised and entrusted to the laity; the Bible, when it is read and not hidden, makes the people feel more liberated, freer and closer to the priest, even though they have not studied as much as he.'

(vi) The new liturgy is neither the traditional Roman Catholic liturgy nor the 'stylised liturgy' of the post-Vatican II specialists. Religious festivals are no longer the domain of the landlord; they belong to the people, who reinterpret them within the context of their daily struggles.

(vii) The concept of God and of religion is re-interpreted. 'From a vindictive God who was up in the clouds, now He is understood as being present with each person, inspiring and changing our lives; from being distant, now God is known as one who accompanies us and Jesus is our brother.'[10]

Being the church, belonging to one another, being active participants, being responsible together for the church, discovering the power and relevance of the Bible, renewal of worship, and a personal relationship with God: are these not all authentic marks of the Holy Spirit? Are they true of our local churches? Of our small groups?

## Losing the vitality

It would be wrong to paint the grassroots communities in too glowing colours. They can and do lose the warmth of the Holy Spirit's presence as much as any church. The faith of the people runs low, if not dry. Recently in Guatemala, where at the end of 1982 there has been violent civil war, several grassroots communities amongst the local Indians in remote regions of the northern region have been compelled to move from village to village because of the violence between guerillas and government forces. Catholic priests have long since had to leave the region, but charismatic renewal in preceding years has proved a source of lifegiving spirituality in circumstances of extraordinary pressure and testing.

No doubt spiritual aridity is as common an experience in the grassroots communities as anywhere else. Maintaining the glow of the Spirit is a challenge faced by every church, and there is no guaranteed formula for success. The interaction of Christians in the closeness of a grassroots community or a home church is the best context available. It is 'the very best sprinkling-machine.'

That is also the conviction of Dr. Paul Yonggi Cho, pastor of the Full Gospel Central Church in Seoul.[11] Cho openly and unequivocally declares that the real secret of church growth is home cell groups. These home cells began in 1964 when Cho was desperately ill and could not carry out the demanding ministry of being the traditional kind of omni-competent pastor. When the laymen of his church proved unwilling to take responsibility for the home cells, Cho turned — against all Korean social conventions — to the women of the church. He remained a very sick man for 10 years, during which time the cells went through many ups and downs. Still, they continued to grow in number and quality. Writing in November 1980, he comments on their life in this way:

'Each week these members gather in their neighbourhood cell meetings, where they have an opportunity to worship the Lord, to pray together, to learn from the Word, to experience the working of the gifts of the Holy Spirit, so see miracles and healings, and to enjoy loving relationships with their fellow-Christians.'[12]

## The fellowship of the Holy Spirit

Now that the ingredients of the home cells have settled down, more freedom is allowed than in the first years of their existence. Members are encouraged to use specific gifts of the Spirit for building up the faith of those present. Cho also stresses the vital importance of each Christian developing a personal relationship with the Holy Spirit, depending on his guidance and leading in faith, not on the leader of the home cell. In this priority, also, there seems to have been growth into maturity; earlier days saw far tighter patterns of leadership and discipleship.

Cho is unashamedly charismatic, although he cannot be conveniently labelled and placed in any box. It is relatively simple to place question-marks against some of his theological emphases — for example, in the area of healing and material prosperity; or in his distinction between '*logos*', as the general Word of God, and '*rhema*' as the revealed Word of God to an individual. But his total openness to and dependence on the Holy Spirit is undeniable and remarkable. He also insists that the leaders of all home cells must 'be filled with the Holy Spirit and guided by the Holy Spirit . . . and have real *fellowship* with the Holy Spirit.'[13] He illustrates this from his own life:

'I felt I had all the diplomas needed to be a preacher in my denomination (i.e. Assemblies of God). I was born again, I had received the baptism in the Holy Spirit, and I had spoken in tongues. So that's all I need, I said to myself. But God changed my attitude and showed me that the Holy Spirit is a person, a person who lives inside me. To live with a person means to have fellowship with that person. . . . It means intimate fellowship and communication.'[14]

Thus, Cho makes fellowship with the Holy Spirit top priority in his daily life, enjoying his presence and encouragement in reading the Bible, preparing for and actually preaching, in prayer — particularly in prayer, because 'this kind of fellowship with the Holy Spirit signifies a life of prayer.' Prayer is an integral part of the home cell meetings, in the conviction that it is through prayer alone that God moves in power.

Eileen Vincent wrote 'God Can Do It Here' after spending some time in the Full Gospel Central Church. She talks of Cho's dependence on the Spirit in vivid terms.

'After considering all the principles expounded by Yonggi

Cho and even wholeheartedly following them, there still will be no growth unless God steps in through the power of the Holy Spirit. . . . Yonggi Cho's faith is not in his own abilities or the principles he has learned through hard experience over the years, but in God himself, by the power of the Holy Spirit. He actively honours the Holy Spirit, and lovingly welcomes him to meetings. . . . Because the Holy Spirit is so honoured, loved, obeyed and respected in the fellowship of the church, he moves amongst them in power. Many mighty acts, miracles, signs, wonders and other visible evidences of God's blessing in the church have caused amazing growth. It is known that God is with his people and he appears to enjoy being there. Although the unconverted don't really understand, it is the Holy Spirit who is the central attraction. It is his peace, joy and love they feel. . . . It is his ministry of encouragement that assures them that their needs can be met. By the power of the Holy Spirit the church grows and grows.'[15]

In the home cells of this remarkable church, Christians receive 'the water which is the faith of the people, and the sun which is the Spirit of God.' When faith interacts with the Spirit of God in this community of love, we have the ingredients for divine action on an unprecedented scale. In very different ways, the grassroots communities of Latin America and the home cell units of Seoul bring us the same inspiration and the same challenge.

'It is only as small churches grow from seeds the Holy Spirit has sown, and with the resources he alone provides, that they will prosper within themselves and fulfil their proper role in congregational life. All too often the introduction of such groups is stage-managed from the top in typical administrative fashion. So parish maps are consulted, catchment areas or lists of names are drawn up, leaders are appointed prior to their commencing, decisions made as to what they shall do and so on. Something may come out of all this activity, but it certainly will not be what we have been talking about. What generally happens is this: several groups run for a while then wither, a couple barely manage to survive, one really comes good. And the majority of people are well and truly insulated against ever attempting anything similar again. No, the real thing begins quite differently, in discerning prayer to see where the Spirit is really preparing the way. This may only be among a small number of people. Then it is a case of tending that, giving it room to grow, at its own pace, in its own way and out of its own resources. It means being content with small beginnings and being prepared to wait for others to catch the same vision before proceeding further. Throughout, it remains an organic, not contrived, affair. Furthermore, the possibility that such tiny initiatives may eventually reshape the life and structures of the whole congregation ought not to be ruled out. We dare not erect fences to hold back the Spirit.'[16]

# Green beans, peppers and mayonnaise

*'A good salad isn't just made of lettuce. It has in it potatoes, green beans, carrots, peppers and mayonnaise. And that is what should happen in the church, it ought to be able to make the most of the qualities and work of each person so as to give a chance to all.'*

Churches in general struggle to motivate and mobilise their members in Christian ministry. The gifts of countless believers lie dormant, even undiscovered, because they are given no genuine opportunity to use them. A few church members will find themselves heavily involved, and they will run the danger of being over-busy, gradually becoming exhausted Christians who can be very disillusioned, if not rather cynical, about ministry as a whole. Others — normally the majority in a congregation — will be content to remain not much more than pewsitters, not necessarily out of any unwillingness to get involved, but because they cannot see where their gifts fit in or because nobody actually knows them well enough to see the value of their contribution.

One of the extra problems when a church begins to grow to any size is the need to man its activities and organisations. In most churches the leaders are looking all the time for people to fill gaps in the programme — two more Sunday School teachers, a youth leader, somebody to run the meetings for older women, a treasurer, a secretary, a coordinator of catering. Anyone who seems a likely candidate is approached, asked to consider the need, and basically expected to slot into the system. In most cultures the same kind of programme, the same organisations and activities, are repeated from church to church. The same gaps must be filled, and people are made to fill holes.

## The overworked few

It is not surprising that this attitude to Christian ministry produces a comparative minority who are run off their feet trying to keep the system going. Most people end up doing more than one job, while others feel like spare parts and excluded from the inner circle of 'church workers'. As the Christians of the Vitoria grassroots communities say, 'the church ought to be able to make the most of the qualities and work of each person, so as to give a chance to all.' That will never happen so long as a congregation does not break down into the kind of small units which bring each individual into a context where he is known, appreciated, encouraged and released into Christian service according to his God-given abilities. This itself means a radical re-think about church organisation. Instead of starting with a fixed programme of activities and meetings, into which leaders squeeze as many members as possible, we need to start with the people themselves, ask what their gifts are, encourage them to develop and use them, and allow the life of the church to grow spontaneously out of those gifts.

Home churches are the most effective way of facilitating this approach to ministry. If, however, they are truly home *churches*, not just groups in the church, we can expect biblical methods of enabling ministry to be used. It is clear, for example, from Paul's teaching in Ephesians that God has given certain people to the church 'to equip the saints for the work of ministry.'[1] Traditionally, these people — apostles, prophets, evangelists, pastors and teachers — have been seen as resources for the larger church, at least the local congregation. If the New Testament truly does envisage the home church as the fundamental unit, as a microcosm of the church and its most visible local manifestation, why should we not expect this five-fold enabling ministry to be present in *each* home church? Is this not what Paul himself understood?

## Crippling elitism

Our major problem is that we have, over the centuries, professionalised these five ministries — even to the extent of combining them all in the vocation of one individual in each congregation, i.e. the clergyman. Of course, there are theological arguments about the authenticity of post-apostolic apostles and post-New Testament prophets. But, if Paul's understanding of the church means anything, it means that these five ministries are essential for building the church in any situation in every generation. Our traditions have turned them into an elite, and this elitist mentality is crippling the mission and growth of the church. If home churches really are home churches, then they contain — at least in embryo — these five ministries, without which they cannot grow up into maturity. But if these five are present, then each home church has the potential resources to grow up into Christ in all things, in every way.

## 48 hours at leisure

A good way to test this possibility is to take a small group of ordinary Christians, perhaps one already in existence so that the knowledge they have of one another can be used effectively, and to set each person this exercise.

'Imagine you have 48 hours completely to yourself — no responsibilities at home, at work, at church; nothing to catch up on, nothing hanging over you; no limitations through illness or family obligations. In such a blissful situation, what would you *choose* to do with those 48 hours, if you really followed your heart's desire?'

Some will immediately respond: 'At last I can get alone with the Lord, rid myself of all the busy-ness and preoccupations of daily living, and listen — listen to what God wants to say to me. I know he has been trying to get through for ages and I have never made the time to be alone with him.' Those who see this as the priority in their hearts have the beginnings of a prophetic ministry. They are prepared to take time to listen to God and to speak out what they hear. This sensitivity to the voice of God, this sense of immediacy in what God wants to say to us, is at the heart of both O.T. and N.T. prophecy.[2] Although every Christian needs to cultivate this sensitivity to the voice of God, the Holy Spirit gives to certain believers the ability and the desire to listen in distinctive measure. Paul wanted everyone in the church at Corinth to prophesy, but he recognized that God would use a few in a special way.

There will be others who will also want to get quietly away for 48 hours, but they will relish the opportunity of getting to grips with the Bible: 'So far I have been skating over the surface: here at last is the opportunity to study something at depth.' They will soak up Paul's letter to the Philippians, become really excited about it and on returning buttonhole the first person they meet: 'Have you seen this great verse in Philippians 3? . . .' That is the beginning of a teaching ministry. Every Christian needs to be a thorough student of the Bible, but a few will be given special enthusiasm for the insight into its riches: these will be able to make the book live to their fellow-Christians in a way that really builds up the body.

A third reaction to the same exercise will invariably be something like this: 'I have been worried about Bill recently; we have not seen much of him around the place, and I sense he may be having a hard time. I'll visit him and cheer him up. Then there's Diana . . . and George . . . and I really must see Dick and Deborah.' This propensity for spending time with individuals, other Christians in need of encouragement or support, is the hallmark of the pastoral ministry. Again, it is incumbent upon every believer to care for other members of Christ's body in all kinds of ways. But the Holy Spirit motivates and equips a few people specifically to be pastors. There may well be rather more pastors in a church than the other four, such is the economy of God.

There will, however, be those whose reaction to 48 hours' free time takes a totally different tack: 'All these religious meetings are a waste of time. Christian in-talk switches me off. All I want to do is to go down to the club or the pub and tell these unbelievers all about the Lord. There's nothing better than a good bit of uncluttered witnessing to out and out pagans — I wish they knew the Lord, just how much he loves them.' That, obviously, is the mark of the budding evangelist. Every Christian should be bubbling over with the goodness of God and always ready to speak about Jesus to others. But not every Christian is called to be an evangelist; certain people are manifestly gifted in a unique way for this ministry, and it is almost as natural as breathing to talk about Jesus. Such Christians are also gifted in pushing enquirers over the edge into personal commitment. Evangelists are obvious when you live close to them.

Prophets, pastors, teachers, evangelists — I had reached this point in the discussion with an Episcopal clergyman in the diocese of Virginia, when he laughingly interrupted with the words: 'All I want to do is to build with bricks: I always have done, since I was a little boy.' Now the fascinating fact about this man was that God has used him in a remarkable way — which amazes him as much as anybody — to plant a new church in that area. He is a church-builder, in the proper sense of the word: not erecting buildings, but bringing into being a lively manifestation of the body of Christ. That is the essence of an apostolic ministry, once the distinctives of full-blooded, Pauline apostleship have been extracted. An apostle is used by the Holy Spirit to break new ground, to plant churches where they do not yet exist. To do that, you have to be able to 'build with bricks.' Such people would spend the 48 hours dreaming of what might be; not daydreaming or on a personal ego-trip, but wondering before God what might be possible if. . . . Now every Christian needs to have an element of this adventuring spirit, the attitude of the pioneer who refuses to settle down in familiar places and methods. Paul reflected it clearly in his ambition to travel to Spain with the gospel, because he was imbued with the desire to preach the gospel where Christ had not yet been named as Lord.[3]

## In every Home Church?

In affirming that these five ministries would be present in virtually any home church, I am not suggesting that in every Christian there is the potential to become one of the five. It is also obvious that these ministries are in no sense watertight compartments: some will swing between one and another; others will have strong inclinations in more than just one direction. We also need to stress that God in his wisdom sometimes calls us out of one ministry into another, either temporarily or permanently. That happens sometimes because he has other work for us to do, or because we have begun to regard that ministry as our ministry, not the Holy Spirit's entrusted to us for the good of the church.

The major point about expecting this five-fold ministry to emerge in the home church situation is this: the ascended Christ has given these ministries to certain people, in order that the body of Christ as a whole might grow up into maturity. An essential feature of such maturity is the freedom of each part to function properly.[4] In other words, these five ministries enable everybody else to recognize and to use their gifts. That is why they are called *enabling* ministries. If we want each person in the church to make the most of their gifts and abilities, each one must be realistically exposed to the enabling ministry of apostles, prophets, evangelists, pastors and teachers. That can happen — and will happen — in the home church context.

It is, incidentally, plain from the New Testament that at certain times most — if not all — of these five ministries were itinerant as well as local. This is certainly true of apostles, prophets and teachers.[5] Where there is a network of home churches in a locality, there is no reason why these enabling ministries should not be shared around according to need. We should beware of creating another elite, which quenches the Spirit's desire to call forth those ministries in every home church. At the same time experience shows that teachers produce teachers, prophets produce prophets, evangelists beget evangelists, etc. It is good, therefore, to expose members of home churches to more developed ministries, so that their own appetite is whetted and their vision enlarged.

It goes without saying that home churches — and local churches — need all five enabling ministries. Otherwise their life becomes lopsided. If there are too many teachers and no evangelists, the church becomes fat and cerebral. If there are no prophets, it stagnates and settles down into comfortable respectability, even complacency. If it is overloaded with evangelists and there is a shortage of pastoral care, the pace will become frenetic and guilt-ridden. If it is all prophets, it gets out of control. A balanced team of enabling ministers will bring out the very best in a church, be it in a home or a local congregation. Only in this way will the rich variety in each church be released.

Most of this discussion is best understood when specifically applied to the times when house churches gather together. The life of a home church is more than its times together. Biblically, the church is called to be the church 24 hours a day, seven days a week. The home church has the same vocation, and the five-fold enabling ministry will facilitate obedience to that vocation. On the other hand, the specific times when the members come together are of crucial importance. This is when its life is focused. What takes place at its meetings will both reflect and determine the people's witness for the rest of the week. If we choose to concentrate on the gifts of each member, and if we allow the five special ministries to take the lead in fostering these gifts, who ends up actually leading the meeting? Before answering this essential question on a pragmatic or experiential basis, let us continue to look closely at Paul's teaching about gifts and ministries.

### Who actually takes the lead?

In 1 Corinthians 12:28 he gives a list of the people whom God has appointed in the church. One group is called 'administrators'. This translation is favoured in virtually every English version of the Bible. However, although the Roman Empire of the first century was no stranger to efficient administration, it is very unlikely that the word Paul uses has the connotation we now give to it with our modern understanding of administrative skills. The Greek word, *kuberneseis*, means 'helmsman' or, more precisely, 'acts of helmsmanship'. Paul has in mind, therefore a person who steers the ship. The helmsman is the one who knows the times of the day and the year, the sky, the stars, the current, the winds. He is the one qualified to direct the ship. 'The literal meaning of the word and its attested usage make it clear what Paul has in mind . . . The reference can only be to the specific gifts which qualify a Christian to be a helmsman to his congregation, i.e. a true director of its order and of its life . . . The importance of a helmsman increases in a time of storm. The office of directing a congregation may well have developed especially in emergencies both within and without. The proclamation of the Word was not originally one of its tasks. The apostles, prophets and teachers saw to this.'[6]

## God's helmsman

God has appointed such helmsmen in his church, in every local church and each home church. This person knows both the others on board and the waters through which they are moving; he knows the signs of danger and he knows where they are heading. He knows who to call on when. He is sensitive to the needs of each situation and to the abilities of each individual. He can, therefore, keep the ship on course and make the best possible use of every person. It is good to remember that there are no passengers on board, only those on active service. If he fails to mobilise anyone's gifts, he will not get very far.

Each home church needs to take note of the person whom God has appointed to serve the body in this way. This man or woman should be clearly entrusted with the task for which God has appointed him or her. This person is unlikely to be someone with one of the five-fold enabling ministries, although those with pastoral gifts might well also have gifts of helmsmanship. It is interesting to note that, in 1 Corinthians 12:28, Paul mentions apostles, prophets and teachers, but he does not refer to pastors. Certainly it is true that pastorally-orientated Christians make far better helmsmen/directors of the life of a church than prophets, teachers or evangelists. However, let us carefully protect the helmsman from the burdens of administration — a task which is far better accomplished by those whom Paul calls 'helpers'. Those who are people-orientated (like helmsmen and pastors) must be protected from administrative responsibilities — for every-one's sake, because the body of Christ will become hard and crusty without pastoral care and wise, sensitive helms-manship. Equally, it will become chaotic and slipshod without efficient administration.

This important ministry will operate in the general life of a home church, and specifically when it gathers together for its weekly meeting. The one at the helm will sense what contribu-tion is needed from whom and what time. Encouragement will be given in particular to those who are reticent about their gifts or are generally shy. He will be sensitive to the way the Spirit is blowing and will do everything possible to catch the full wind of the Spirit. He will sense when some word from the Lord is needed or imminent, making space for it to be received, weighed and absorbed. He will call for some clear biblical teaching when folk seem to be floundering in a welter of private opinions. All the time he will be working to keep the meeting on course, not in the direction he wants it to go but as he senses the Spirit wants to take it. He will be constantly listening to the suggestions of others, without taking his eye off the Lord. Such helmsmanship skills take time to develop. They are needed in every aspect of the church's life — steering worship and decision-making are two major areas.

So who actually ends up leading the meeting of the home church? The Holy Spirit, as he guides the helmsman to make full use of the gifts and ministries of every member. If it is true that all that is needed to be the church is present in embryo in each home church, it stands to reason that in practice we need to start from where we are, steadily moving forward towards attaining what at present may be no more than a vision in front of us, particularly when the going is tough or pedestrian. We look for the evidence of what God has already given in the people with whom we are already linked — if we belong to some kind of home group already. Or we start from scratch in a new group in the same conviction that God can make of this collection of individuals an authentic manifestation of his church.

## An example from Chile

It is important to consider at least one example of home church life, which already shows clear signs of moving towards this reality. The situation, already referred to, in Portezuelo, Chile, provides a rewarding illustration.[7] Eighteen grassroots communities make up the parish, and each community has a small 'council', consisting of eight people or certainly covering eight areas of ministry. These are:

(i)    *Coordinator*: presides over the community and ensures that each member uses his/her gifts in Christian service.

(ii)   *Animator of the Community*: directs the meetings and Sunday worship.

(iii)   *Animator of Family Catechetics*: prepares and trains the families, meetings with them once a week to teach them in such a way that they can form their own children in Christ.

(iv)   *Animator of Youth Groups*: directs all the activities amongst older young people.

(v)    *Animator of Children's Groups*: supervises pastoral and teaching ministry to the children, organizing special events.

(vi)   *Animator of Community Action*: organizes and coordinates activities of all kinds to help the needy.

(vii)  *Head of Finances*: organizes programme of tithing, administers the material goods of the community, and sends accounts to central parish council.

(viii) *Animator of Work with Married Couples*: responsible both for preparing engaged couples and for giving further instruction to those who have completed family catechetics (iii).

Here is a wide range of ministry, requiring many gifts from many people. Each grassroots community in the parish has this kind of involvement, because each is the church in its particular area. The Portezuelo communities appear to be somewhat larger than others, nearer to the maximum of 15 families allowed in the home cells of the church in Seoul. Obviously, sheer size — or the lack of it — will have a lot of influence on what each home church can express in terms of being the church. We must be careful not to let these mechanics of operation blind us to this one simple fact: none of the communities depends entirely on a simple gifted individual to sustain their group existence. Shared responsibility is structured into their organization, and this broad distribution of tasks clearly contributes to the vitality of each community. No plain lettuce salad here.

# CHAPTER 6

# Thousands of yellow Volkswagens

*'There are thousands of yellow Volkswagens in Brazil, but every owner knows perfectly well which is his because, although the cars all look alike, each has its own peculiar characteristics. Our church, likewise, ought to have its own special features, its own qualities, its particular way of operating.'*

We need to take the theme of variety further. If it is right to let the life of a church grow out of the distinctive gifts of each member, rather than squeezing the members into the pre-planned programme of the church, then each home church is going to be different. It will have 'its own special features, its own qualities, its particular way of operating.' Naturally, there will be similarities — characteristics of God's church in every culture and generation. Hopefully, these are more attractive than Volkswagens! Any network of home churches in a parish will, therefore, have a great variety within it. In fact, one of the greatest temptations in starting home churches is to impose the same characteristics on them, instead of allowing something distinctive to grow out of the coming-together of different people.

The original home cells in Seoul were very strictly and heavily controlled. The biblical teaching was handed out to the leaders (it still is); the time to be spent together was laid down; the other ingredients were clearly stipulated. Although the home cells today are more flexible and varied, Korean (and Asian) culture imposes a certain rigidity on them which would probably grate on those accustomed to more personal freedom.

At the same time, if there is genuine interdependence between the home churches in a parish, it will be in order and highly constructive to have a measure of common features. One of the most effective ways is to tie in the Sunday preaching to the whole congregation with the Bible study in the home churches. This encourages unity and also gives far more substance to the pulpit ministry, which can so easily be so many words into the air. One of the most dangerous aspects of much Western Christianity, particularly amongst evangelicals, is the plethora of words: often the teaching is good and thorough. But it has no context for practical obedience. We hear sermon after sermon; we listen to tape after tape; we have Bible study after Bible study. And scarcely any of it is put into practice. We think about it; we absorb it in our minds; but that is where it stays. The danger of this syndrome comes from its spiritual impact on us. To hear God's Word without putting what what we hear into practice is counterproductive, according to Jesus.[1]

## Practical obedience

The home church is the ideal context for working out the practical implications of God's Word. The most practically-minded preacher can do no more than give examples of how a particular part of God's Word will apply to the lives of those who hear him. We need the more personal, discipling atmosphere of the home church to follow it through with each individual. A network of home churches operating with the same material along these lines will have a great diversity of life.

There will naturally be times when a local congregation will need to have straight teaching throughout its home churches. This will best be done in the smaller context, rather than from the pulpit. It could be placed in the hands of those with teaching gifts in each home church, or those thus gifted could move around the home churches. A very effective way is to circulate the teaching on tape or on video. The latter medium, in particular, could well become a unique tool for binding together the home churches of a congregation. It is ideal for communicating particular prayer needs, passing on information from the centre, giving study outlines, bringing anything of immediate importance to the home churches.

The way a biblical theme for a whole parish takes on individual distinctiveness in one particular home church is well illustrated in this story from the diocese of Vitoria. Padre Lute is the priest of the parish in the Oriente area. There are ten grassroots communities in his parish, which has almost ceased to exist except as an administrative concept in Canon law. All decisions are taken by the communities. All liturgical preparation, instruction for the sacraments, visiting and counselling is done within the communities. Finance is totally under the control of the communities. Every Monday the leaders of the communities meet to reflect on the gospel and plan the week's work. In this parish a visitor recorded the following:

## One Brazilian example

'The theme that fortnight was that Jesus was born poor and humble and shares our life: the question was 'why?' The women present were all poor. None had had much formal education. Most were migrants from rural areas. All knew real hardship. They could easily identify with a poor family on the move whose baby had been born in a stable. Indeed, a one-minute reading of St. Luke's account of the nativity provoked a one-hour discussion of the injustices, humiliations and hardships that the mothers themselves experienced.

'They discussed the terrible health services available in the area and how a local woman's baby had been born while she was waiting in the queue to see the doctor (the baby died). They swapped accounts of having to wait in shops while better-dressed people were served first and how as domestic servants they were treated without respect by their mistresses. They talked of the high price of food in the local shops. . . .

'After an hour the catechist put the question: "Why did Jesus choose to be born poor and humble?" "Maybe," said one woman, a mother of ten of whom three had died and only two were working, "maybe it was to show these rich people that we are important too."

'A ripple of excitement went through the room. Was God really making such a clear statement about *their* humanity? About *their* rights as people? The discussion progressed, but with an electric charge in the air. Half an hour later a young woman said, 'I think we still haven't got the right answer to the first question.' A complete hush. 'I think,' she went on, 'that God chose his son to be born like us so that we can realize that we are important. It is not just to show the bosses. It is to show us too!'

'And suddenly I saw what it means to say that the gospel has the power to set people free . . . For these women, fired by a sudden consciousness of their own worth, of their identification with Jesus Christ, by an awareness of God's love for them . . . these women went on to discuss what they should be doing about the high food prices, about how a particular chain of shops had cornered the market and was overcharging, and how they themselves would link up with other catechetic groups and grassroots communities across the sector to organise a boycott.'[2]

## Expecting the unexpected

This Brazilian example underlines what the Australian writer, Robert Banks, has called the 'surprising quality'[3] of church life as envisaged and described by Paul in the New Testament. 'There was to be a readiness for the unexpected whenever Christians meet together. Whatever may have happened in these gatherings of a more or less regular kind, they were always to remain open to the unpredictable.' This openness guarantees diversity. Without advocating any kind of disorderliness,[4] Paul wanted the home churches (as much if not more than the whole local church) to be 'open to the Lord's intervention whenever and wherever he is willing to interfere.'[5] It is surprisingly difficult to maintain this attitude of openness to God, particularly if we are trained to be orderly and to plan ahead Most Westerners are thus programmed: hence the richness of the insights available to us from Latin America and Africa. We have clocks and watches built into our sub-conscious. In some parts of Latin America, the phrase used to stress the importance of keeping punctually to an appointment is 'hora inglesa' i.e. 'English time'! Africans also speak of 'European time'. We also feel we know what needs to be included in any gatherings of the church. Without jettisoning the strength of this attitude, we need to press ahead with initiatives which make for spontaneity and which create space for the unexpected. It is far more important to hear what God is saying to us, than to complete the programme. One of the simplest ways to encourage such surprises is by using silence.

## Open to needy people

Another aspect of this surprising quality of church life, according to Banks, is 'an ever-present openness to those in the greatest need, accompanied by a willingness to drop everything else, however important it may have seemed, so that the fullest attention and help can be given. The test of any community is whether it can recognize that moment and, when it arrives, be able to devote its concentrated energies to it.'[6]

The home church is ideally placed to take such opportunities for personal ministry. On countless occasions someone has suddenly blurted out a deep hurt or anxiety in such a context. Unless it clearly requires specialist care in a more confidential setting, that is precisely the opportunity for the church to be the church to and with the person in need. We can rely on the Holy Spirit in such a situation to distribute all the gifts needed for the grace of God to bring wholeness, comfort and healing. It does not require any self-conscious or 'heavy' approach. The net result will be that all experience God's grace in a new way. Each leaves the place richer than when they came in.

Such potential for unique experiences of being the church is resident in any home church which is prepared, allowed and expected to be fully responsible for its life together. If there is constant checking-out by the local leadership, in a paternalistic and untrusting way, there will always be a feeling of inhibition and restraint. This comes back to the question of giving home churches the freedom to grow up into maturity, not abandoning them to their own devices on the one hand nor dictating what they should do on the other. We will look at the details of this in the last chapter. For the time being let us recognize that 'beyond a certain size, meetings become too regulated for God or the desperately needy to break in on our consciousness in any radical way, and too dominated by a few to allow everyone to play a part in determining the community's affairs.'[7]

## The gifts of each individual

One of the obvious ways in which the distinctiveness of each home church can be encouraged is by deliberately taking time to let each individual talk about themselves; not in the sense of encouraging them to dump all their emotional garbage on the rest (as happens in some secular groups) or to engage in constant introspection, but by discouraging anything but openness and honesty. The Quakers have four questions which they use in starting groups, which could be of great value in some places:

(i)     Where did you live between the ages of 7 and 12? How many brothers and sisters did you have at the time?
(ii)    How did you heat your home at that time?
(iii)   Where in your home at that time was the centre of human warmth?
(iv)    When, if ever, in your life did God become more than just a word?[8]

From time to time it is important to encourage the home church as a whole to evaluate the distinctive gifts in each individual. Normally it requires the relaxed environment and schedule of a weekend away to make this really profitable. In fact, the value of such time away together can hardly be exaggerated. It is worth doing right at the outset, when the group first gets off the ground. In such a context the whole ethos of the home church can be spelt out and experienced. It often takes many evening weekly sessions to progress half as far. It is probably good to have such time away twice a year: if a congregation of some size has several such home churches, it is worth considering the possibility of investing in a suitable property for such a priority (probably along with other congregations in the area).

The grassroots communities in the diocese of Nova Iguaca in Brazil have been asked the following four questions on a regular basis, in order to evaluate their life and work as individual communities:

(i)     What is your community doing that is good?

(ii) What is your community doing and could do better?
(iii) What is your community doing and should not be doing?
(iv) What is your community not doing and should be doing?[9]

If all the home churches in a congregation are to follow through such an exercise on a regular basis, the diversity and unity of the body of Christ would both be greatly strengthened. After all, even Volkswagen have launched out into a wide range of models.

# CHAPTER 7

# Stagnant water breeds insects

*'Stagnant water breeds insects. It is bad for health. But running water is clean, anyone can drink it. A church which is turned in upon itself . . . cannot slake the thirst which men have for God.'*

It is time to move explicitly into the outward mission of the home churches. We have already noted the way so many small groups become turned in on themselves, shrivel and die. When spiritual growth is seen as an end in itself, this will invariably happen. The mission of home churches is nothing less than the mission of the whole church. Therefore, home churches will grow or die according to their response to the missionary call of God.

It hardly needs saying that Christians alone can point the way to 'slake the thirst men have for God.' What may not be quite so plain is that the home church, when its arms and heart are turned outward into the local community, will find itself scratching many people precisely where they itch. They are looking urgently for some experience of true belonging in a small group.

One of the most recent trends in New Testament theology has been to examine 'the social matrix out of which the documents arose,'[1] with the goal of discovering the social world of apostolic Christianity. Robert Banks' book *Paul's Idea of Community*[2] devotes its first chapter to the social and religious setting of the New Testament churches. Banks makes it clear that precisely the same longing for community characterised the world of the Mediterranean basin in Paul's day. 'His idea of community touched the raw nerve of certain changes taking place in first-century Hellenistic society,'[3] says Banks and pinpoints three clamant needs which the early Christian communities met in a remarkable way.

## The raw nerve of contemporary society

First, many people were searching for a more intimate form of family or communal life. Both Jew and Greek had traditionally found a sense of identity and purpose in his family, especially if he happened to be the head of it. Because both Jewish and Greek family life was not based on the nuclear model but on the extended family, the responsibilities involved and the variety of interests implicit in such a role had been adequate for providing a sense of identity and purpose. But this left everyone who was not head of a household in a very loose and unfulfilled position, notably slaves and other various dependants, adults who remained unmarried and the outcasts of society.

The second need arose out of general disillusionment with the relevance of national and local politics. For Greeks the city-state democracy of fifth century Athens was a distant memory. There were still opportunities for those keen on public service of some kind, but the influence of Roman imperialism had for some time drastically reduced the actual scope for political significance. True power now lay in the hands of a small minority, who were naturally reluctant either to spread it very far or hand it on to others. In most places, the harsh reality of Roman garrisons and Roman governors overshadowed any local exercise of power. In any case, there had always been those without votes or rights in both Greek and Jewish society; as in every generation, these people longed for a place where they counted and they could say what they liked without fear or favour.

In addition to this political disillusionment, there was a search for something which transcended any and every form of exclusivism — parochial, tribal and national divisions were deplored by an increasing number of Jews and Greeks. The Jews looked forward to an international theocracy ruled by the Messiah from Jerusalem, while many Greeks were fascinated by the Stoic dream of the universal commonwealth of nations where peace and justice would reign.

The third need was more directly spiritual, the cry of the heart for spiritual reality: something supernatural, beyond the simply material things of life. Together with this hunger went a thirst for ordinary human warmth and friendship, to break down the anonymity of a monotonous daily routine. The old religions had had their day; they had been tried and found wanting.

These three needs in first-century society naturally spawned any number of possible solutions. Relatively few were gripped by the rather abstract dreams of Stoic philosophers: the mood amongst ordinary Jews was one of resignation, if not scepticism, towards the prospect of the Messiah ushering in a new life — you had to be something of a Pharisee to keep the Messianic hope burning after generations of foreign occupation and centuries of prophetic promises. What did happen at that time was the emergence of 'a variety of voluntary associations that multiplied in cities all over the ancient world . . . They attracted a wide following — in part from the socially disadvantaged members of society . . . They bound together people from different backgrounds on a different ground to that of geography and race, or natural and legal ties. Their principle was *koinonia*, i.e. a voluntary sharing or partnership.'[4]

## Clubs and guilds

The majority of these clubs and societies were organised around a particular interest, vocation or commitment. They were extremely varied: political, military and sporting; professional and commercial fields; artisans and craftsmen of different kinds; philosophical schools and religious brotherhoods. They varied in size from ten to one hundred, but mostly averaged around 30–35. A particular kind of such a club or society was the *thiasos*, a private cultic group involved in one or other of the Greek mystery religions, which abounded in Greek cities at the time. Worship was given to foreign deities such as Cybele, Attis, Isis, Osiris, Adonis and Mithras. In many ways the *thiasoi* provided a full, if not actually satisfying, milieu for searching materialists. The cults were centred on highly dramatic ritual and initiated members into vivid mystical experiences. They opened their doors to men of all nationalities, and to women and slaves as well. A particular fascination lay in the secrecy enjoined on their adherents.

If this was, indeed, the social world of the first century, it is not surprising that the newly-emerging Christian communities found themselves in a position to make real inroads into the world of their contemporaries. The home churches met all three basic needs: The sense of being the family of God was fundamental to their life together; they called one another brothers and sisters, they knew God as Father and Jesus as elder Brother. To know God through Jesus Christ was to enter a family whose ties transcended even the closest bonds between members of one's earthly family. But home churches were not just extended families; they had work to do, service to fulfil, responsibilities to shoulder — and their membership was comprised of all sorts and conditions of men — Jew and Greek, rich and poor, slaves and free, male and female, educated and uneducated. So, to a true sense of belonging was added a sense of having a job to do in a highly distinctive kind of 'society'. On top of these two characteristics, welding the members together in one fellowship, was spiritual worship of the one, true God. In the fellowship-meal, through psalms and hymns and spiritual songs, with the manifestation of spiritual gifts of all kinds, these home churches offered all the mystery-cults offered, and far more. Thus, for the first-century Christian, the church was part of the gospel he proclaimed: 'Come and see' could easily have been his general invitation to friends, neighbours, relatives and colleagues — because most of them would have tried some social alternative over the years.

In a very strange and fascinating way, it is no different in the world today at the latter end of the 20th century. Clubs, associations and voluntary societies abound in the Western world. Perhaps the biggest single social crisis is the break-up of family life. We are now beyond the relative remoteness of soaring statistics about marriages that have failed. A whole generation is reaching adulthood, amongst whom there are appallingly few who have not been scarred by family break-down of some kind. Living in a university city like Oxford, this is painfully apparent; whereas 20 years ago relatively few students stayed in Oxford beyond the end of term, now a large proportion arrive early and leave late. Increased academic pressure is one reason, but on enquiry it becomes clear that unhappy homes are often the real cause. Amongst such people there is a despairing cry for the kind of family relationships which are uniquely possible in a home church, especially when it is based in a truly Christian home. Young people, in particular, flock to any club or group which offers them a sense of belonging, of being known and valued, and especially of being needed and having work to do.

## Modern longings

Young people also long for a context in which the divisions and hostility between men and nations can be superseded. The idealism and the simplistic solutions they cherish can be seen in movements like the Green Party in West Germany, and in the wider call for nuclear disarmament. If people were able to see in the church a genuine commitment to peace and justice, the gospel would have far greater impact. Home churches cannot afford to sidestep these major issues which haunt today's generation. More positively, they have a wonderful opportunity to commend the gospel to people who long for a community of integrity and relevance.

It is plain that there is a strongly religious yearning in today's world. The increase of different cults and sects has been carefully researched and documented. The evidence for their proliferation is all around us. Again, contact with young people of all kinds bears out the widespread, almost universal, exposure they are given to occult practices and literature. Hunger for supernatural experiences is rampant and it is in effect a hunger for God himself. The peer-group pressure on young people is probably the biggest single factor affecting their daily lives. They club together in many different groups in this need to belong and be recognized.

For these crucial reasons we must work hard, not just to establish home churches throughout our neighbourhood, but to ensure that they provide the context in which this thirst for God can be slaked. This thirst is universal. It can be temporarily quenched with spiritual substitutes or be dulled by material affluence. Where there are few alternatives and no material wealth, the thirsty ones are looking to the Christian church, if it exists. This substantially explains the way the

Latin American grassroots communities have begun to slake the thirst of the poor and disadvantaged. In most countries in Latin America, the ordinary people can look only to the Catholic church for this living water. For centuries they had looked in vain, receiving largely a religious substitute, not the living water of the gospel. Increasingly today the church is not simply out amongst the ordinary people; the church *is* the people.

The needs are obvious. Apart from the overriding need of all men for the forgiveness of God and the new life of the Holy Spirit, mediated through the death and resurrection of Jesus, the poor people of Latin America need to belong, to be valued, to be needed, to press on with the work of securing a just humane and compassionate society. That is the agenda of the grassroots communities, because they have caught the urgency of God's missionary heart. They do not see their life together except in terms of working out their salvation day by day in their local community. That is where God has sent and placed them. There they are being the church. The utter relevance of their lifestyle as grassroots communities issues us with a challenge: is the lifestyle of our church, local or in the home, relevant to the people amongst whom God has sent and placed us? 'Running water is clean, anyone can drink it.'

## One enormous risk

There is — and there always has been — one enormous risk for a church living authentically as a missionary church: because it is responding to God's summons to be fully involved in the world, in the same way as he immersed himself in it in Jesus, it will continuously be on the verge of being contaminated by, if not assimilated to, the world. The grassroots communities walk that tightrope, and there are those who believe that many of them have lost their biblical balance, especially through uncritical espousal of Liberation Theology.[5] Instead of offering water to thirsty people, it is stated, they are providing a substitute which tastes nice, but leaves a nasty taste and cannot slake thirst. The ordinary people are being encouraged in the name of Jesus Christ to stand up for their rights, even to the extent of confronting the powers-that-be (who in most Latin American countries are cynically repressive). In Nicaragua, this has led to members of grassroots communities joining the Sandinista revolution:

'For the first time in Latin American history, not simply individual Christians, but whole Christian communities, have played an important role in a liberation movement, and these same Christians continue to work for the reconstruction of their country.'[6]

If taking up arms in a revolution against the existing government seems totally alien and remote to Christians in the West, the principle of missionary identification by the church with the people amongst whom God has put it must never be lost. Fleshing out that principle will vary from situation to situation. We all run the risk of getting our hands dirty if we are prepared to get our feet wet. Unless we take risks and make mistakes, we will not establish a bridgehead for the gospel. We will remain that living contradiction of the gospel: Christians who shout from their holy ghetto that Jesus is the answer, instead of living in the midst and commending Jesus as Lord by a relevant lifestyle and clear proclamation.

## The use and abuse of the Bible

There is one central and determinative factor which needs our particular attention in pursuing God's call to us to be a missionary church, namely our approach to and use of the Bible. Although we have referred to it from time to time in previous chapters, now is the time to look at the subject in more detail. Not only will we be protected by the Scriptures from serious errors in missionary tactics and methods, we will also — by constant and humble exposure to their teaching — avoid the danger of stagnation in our home churches. Christians who are continuously being stretched by God's Word in their practical discipleship will never stagnate. More positively, the home church which is all the time allowing the Bible to mould its life together in every aspect will be offering running water to the thirsty, without any need to be constantly checking either the watering-system or the proximity of thirsty people.

One of the strongest advantages of the home church is its

opportunity to discover the truth of the Scriptures as a corporate experience: ordinary Christians being led by the Spirit of truth into the truth. In no way do we intend to diminish or undervalue the ministry of those whom God has given to his church as teachers. Their contribution to the discovery of biblical truth is as necessary for the growth of the body into maturity as any other member's gifts. Nevertheless, there is an important way in which the ordinary members of a home church can unlock the meaning of God's Word today.

In all interpretation of the Scriptures there are three aspects which must be held together — the text itself, the historical context to which the text originally applied and in which it was written, and the way it is understood and is to be applied in today's situation. The interaction of these three factors, under the direction of the Holy Spirit, enables us today to hear and to obey God's Word. Normally in today's church the application of today's situation is done by one particular person: that person is trained in a particular way, which may be more or less helpful in arriving at the application of the text to the contemporary world. When the members of a home church wrestle with the text of the Bible in an atmosphere of love for one another and worship of God, the Holy Spirit will make the text come alive in ways inaccessible to the preacher/ teacher on his own. Their life-situations will shed light on the text in a distinctive way, just as the exegetical gifts of the teacher will shed light on its original context and on the meaning of the actual words used.

## A new way of doing Theology

Those involved in the grassroots communities of Latin America see this process as 'a new way of doing theology.'[7] We have grown so accustomed to theological colleges and lecturers, to commentaries and teachers, that we leave theology to the experts. We then complain that their teaching is abstract, unintelligible and irrelevant. One of the foremost theological enablers of the grassroots communities in Brazil, Carlos Mesters, declares his aim as being to re-establish 'contact between the Word of God and the people for whom the Word was intended.'[8] Mesters has a profound respect for the wisdom of the people, what he calls 'sensus fidelium' — i.e. the way 'the people have their antennae hooked up in order to pick up the message of the Bible . . . they already have a door open to enter the world of the Bible.'[9] Mesters sees four interacting elements which register the authority of the Word of God on us — the text of Scripture itself, the ways in which Scripture has been interpreted down the years, the authoritative message of the contemporary teacher, and this 'sensus fidelium'. A few examples, mainly from Mesters' writings, plus excerpts from the resource materials he has provided for grassroots communities, will show the attractive, relevant and powerful way the Bible is being used in their life together. They will also compel us to ask a few leading questions about the way we use the Bible — in general, but particularly in small groups. First, two comments by another 'pastoral agent' of the Brazilian communities, Betto Libanio:

'The difference between the reading that we traditional priests make of the Bible and that which the communities make is that we look at the Bible as though we are looking through a window, curious to see what is happening outside, while the people of the communities look at the Bible as one looks at a mirror, to see a reflection of their own reality. Thus, our reference to the Bible is . . . to bygone things, all very nice, wherein God was present . . . What happens in the communities is completely to the contrary. The people feel as though they are seeing their own lives revealed in the accounts of the Bible . . . The primary task would seem to be one of returning the keys of the Bible back to the people. . . .'[10]

Libanio continues with a pungent comment:

## A lamp to our feet?

'Evangelicals remind me of people who are walking along a dark path with a torch. They are so fascinated by the light that, instead of shining it down and ahead on the path, they point it at themselves . . . staring at it, . . . when they are not aiming it up to heaven! According to the Psalmist, God's Word is a lamp to our *feet* and a light to our *pathway*. You evangelicals are pointing the Bible in the wrong direction!'[11]

Carlos Mesters also has a vivid way of challenging us to

allow the people in home churches to discover the Bible for themselves:

'The people do not exist for exegesis, but exegesis for the people . . . The ultimate purpose of the Bible is not scientific research of its literal and historical meaning, but rather to prepare men for the struggle that is before us (Hebrews 12:1), and to help them to live life to its fullest . . . Exegesis is at times like the gardener who took a famished man to his apple orchard. But instead of giving him some fruit right away so he could eat, he began to talk about the fertilizer and about the roots that would produce the fruit. When he had finished talking, he looked around and couldn't find the famished man. Tired of waiting, the man had left to go and find another orchard, where he began to eat the fruit that the owner gave him . . . The hungry man wasn't interested in the roots nor in the fertilizers. He wanted to satisfy his hunger. Our people are hungry and thirsty and, before anything else, they ask for food for their dwindling hopes.'[12]

Mesters has produced a large amount of biblically-based material for use in the grassroots communities. Where the members are not literate, the study is led from a workbook by someone who is. Otherwise, each member has a booklet and there is a leader's guide. Mesters is concerned to make the Bible live for his people today, in order for them to be able to apply it in their own particular situations. He makes his reflection material practical in a series of ten booklets covering 40 topics in all. Each topic consists of a simple liturgy, a contextual homily, a Scripture text in popular language, and questions for reflection applied to real-life situations. Here are some examples of the questions:

On the Resurrection: 'Jesus rose again in the morning, but for those two lads (i.e. on the road to Emmaus) the resurrection didn't take place until the evening. Has the resurrection arrived for you? Have you found him? Tell us about it.'

On Friendship: 'What was lacking in Geraldo's friendship (in the introductory homily), and in the friendship of Judas and Peter that led them to the point of betraying and denying a friend?'

On the Hope of Resurrection: 'Is it enough to wait for heaven or shouldn't we work to change things down here? Why?'

On Jesus and the Sheep and Goats: ' "You didn't know it, but it was Me! I was walking and you gave me a ride" — if all the good people get saved, what's the use of being a good Catholic?'[13]

To many readers, especially those used to studying the Bible informally in groups, such an approach is familiar and valuable. These examples have been included to substantiate this assessment of the attitude taken to the Bible by the grassroots communities, at least in Brazil —

'Scripture is indeed taken seriously by all those who are involved in the communities. Their interest is not speculative.'[14]

Home churches that allow the Word of God to direct and mould their life will be constantly refreshed in the Lord and will quench many a thirst in friends and neighbours. Only such biblically inspired and controlled mission will last the course, avoid both staleness and substitutes for the living water, and be able to keep on responding to the call of God to compassionate involvement in the local community — and beyond it.

# CHAPTER 8

# Up and down the bus

*'The church is like a bus. No one gets on a bus to walk up and down it, but to be carried from one place to another. A bus is a vehicle, a means of transport . . . The mission of the church doesn't lie within itself, but outside it. It is to proclaim the kingdom of God within the world of men.'*

The last decade or so has seen the church as a whole wrestling with its theology of mission. 'The theology of missions is the central issue where the major controversies among Christians converge.'[1] Catholics and Protestants, from the first and the third world, evangelical and liberal — all are involved. Orlando Costas has written: 'We are experiencing a crisis of wholeness and integrity. The fundamental missiological question before the Christian church is not whether mission should be conceived as vertical, horizontal, or both; not whether it should be thought of either as spiritual and personal, or material and social; nor whether we should emphasize in our practice one aspect or another. It is rather whether we can recover its wholeness and its efficacy, whether we can see it as a whole and live up to its global objectives.'[2]

## The Gospel of the Kingdom

Jesus and the apostles proclaimed the gospel of the kingdom of God[3] — not 'the gospel' or 'the kingdom', but the gospel of the kingdom. Jesus, the King of that kingdom, is the good news we proclaim. When we proclaim him as King, we provoke an encounter with him. Because he is who he is, those who encounter him cannot remain the same: change, or a refusal to change, inevitably occurs. There is clearly a time when individuals either encounter Jesus for the first time or become aware for the first time of encountering Jesus. We believe and pray that this first encounter will produce a radical turn-around in their lives, radical enough to provoke many more turn-arounds every day from that moment onwards. We therefore use every opportunity, every method, to present Jesus, the King to everyone — not just to certain people, but to all, because Jesus is King of kings and Lord of lords. This privilege of evangelism, i.e. sharing the good news of Jesus, is the calling of the church, the mission of the church: we are sent by God into the world to live and preach the gospel.

In this chapter we are concerned with this calling and this privilege as entrusted to home churches. In such a microcosm of the church effective evangelism can be carried out more readily than in virtually any other context. In particular, Costas' call for mission with integrity can be heeded. The home church is ideally placed to proclaim Jesus as King over every aspect of life, to commend him by a corporate life that manifestly demonstrates the power of the Spirit to bring reconciliation and healing, to come alongside those in need in practical compassion and understanding, to answer thoroughly the queries and the worries which people inevitably have about the implications of commitment to Christ, and to graft those who decide to follow Christ into a fellowship of believers who are known and trusted. Other methods of evangelism fall short of these ideals in so many ways.

The challenge to us is whether we know where we are going: i.e. are we enjoying the experience of being in a home church for its own sake, or are we ready to move out at any time at the prompting of the Spirit? The Vitoria document likens the church to a bus. Buses are universal in Latin America: everybody uses them. Visitors who want to sample local colour and life in the raw cannot do better than ride the buses. For a flat fare you can go virtually anywhere in urban areas: it is a fascinating experience. But you need to be ready to get off some time before you reach your destination, otherwise the sheer press of people will take you well past the stop — especially if you are still enjoying the experience of being on the bus! It is like that with evangelism: if we enjoy being together in our home church too selfishly, we will not be ready to share the good news with those outside. We must be on the alert and motivated to seize every opportunity: that means both a heart on fire with the good news and basic equipment to enable us to share it.

We have already noted that certain people have a gift for, if not a distinctive ministry in, evangelism — in the same way as others are teachers or prophets. But every Christian possesses the good news and can testify to it. The member (or members) of a home church who shows distinctive evangelistic gifts will be a very important resource for galvanising and mobilising the church as an evangelistic unit. The priority placed by the local congregation on evangelism will also be fairly determinative. It is very difficult to maintain the zeal for sharing the good news, if there is no such encouragement at the centre. Christians also need to see the impact of the gospel on the lives of unbelievers, to witness the change in people when they encounter Christ and turn to him. In other words, the best way to be trained and motivated in evangelism is to evangelise. There can be little doubt that the Western church, in particular, has been inundated with teaching about evangelism to such an extent that head-knowledge has frequently prevented rather than released actual evangelism. In the love and trust of a home church all can evangelise. If the home church does not evangelise, it dies — indeed, it is not the church in any real sense.

Orlando Costas mentions the slogan of the Evangelism-in-depth programme, which has made such an impact in different countries in Latin America: 'Abundant reaping requires abundant sowing.' He adds: 'We have also come to realize that abundant sowing requires abundant cultivation and, likewise, abundant cultivation demands abundant reaping. Harvest time is a critical period. You run the chance of losing precious fruit. It requires total dedication, a total effort to reap. In Costa Rica's rural communities, when coffee season comes, schools are closed. Children go out into the countryside to pick coffee beans. Everybody is caught up in the process of harvest, because if you don't pick the fruit, there's not going to be anything to eat.'[4]

## Four harvest priorities

Costas identifies four priorities if the harvest is to be effectively reaped: first, intelligent investment of time and energy in spreading the gospel. Secondly, patient cultivation of those who can be mobilised for evangelism and those who are to be evangelised. Thirdly, flexibility in space and methods. Fourthly, sensitivity and sacrificial dedication to the Spirit's movement in people's lives.[5] We will look at each one in turn.

## Intelligent investment

Intelligent investment by members of a home church of time and energy requires, at the very least, that they sit down together and discuss the opportunities, fears and problems they have in sharing the gospel. Evangelism must be on the agenda of the home church — explicitly, consistently, centrally, The Full Gospel Central Church in Seoul is an unprecedented example of this:

'How does a home cell set about winning someone for the Lord? The group gathers and has a brain-storming session. Who, they ask, in their locality or amongst their acquaintances has a problem? They have been taught to look for those in need and then meet that need through the sufficiency they have in Christ. Sickness, problems and heartaches are their opportunity. Rather than running from them, they look for them.'[6]

The church's pastor, Yonggi Cho, also writes about this aspect of home cell life. He begins by downplaying the value of door-to-door evangelism: 'it invites resistance. . . . It's true that many people are saved through door-to-door Christian witnessing, and the Holy Spirit will sometimes motivate Christians to undertake that kind of evangelism in areas where he has already prepared the hearts of the unbelievers. But, in general, door-to-door evangelism becomes frustrating for the Christian witness because he sees such a low rate of productivity.'[7] It may be that Cho has become so accustomed to seeing results, that he can afford to forgo door-to-door visiting, which is always difficult and demanding, in favour of other methods. On the other hand, the strategic investment in time and effort he does endorse may well achieve the same ends in a local community. He calls it 'holy eavesdropping':

'Our cell leaders instruct the members of their group to be

on the lookout for anyone who is having troubles. Many of us overhear conversations every day in which someone is speaking about the problems in his life. Whenever we hear such a conversation, we should immediately ask the Holy Spirit, 'Is there some way in which I can witness to this person. Is there some way I can introduce him to Jesus, who can really solve his problems?' '[8]

Seoul is one of the largest cities in the world and, like any city, has countless high-rise apartment buildings. 'One of our home cell leaders began to spend a few hours every Saturday riding up and down in the elevator of her apartment building. On many of those rides she found opportunities to help people. One mother needed someone to carry her baby; an older woman needed help in carrying her groceries to the apartment. . . . Little by little she became friends with many of the people she helped in the elevator. All the while she was secretly 'planting' a home cell meeting in her apartment building. While she was helping these people and making friends, she was silently praying for them. Eventually she obtained their telephone numbers from them, and she called them to invite them to a cell group meeting in her apartment. She was so successful that today, if you go to any of the high-rise apartment buildings near our church on a Saturday afternoon, you will find our cell leaders in the elevators, riding up and down, up and down. . . .'[9]

Strategic investment of time and energy, therefore, may involve nothing more or less than members of a home church discussing evangelistic opportunities creatively and imaginatively, spending time in prayer (together and individually) for unbelievers known to them (naturally or by 'holy eavesdropping'), and setting aside specific time each week to be in the places where the unbelievers are. For many busy Christians this threefold strategy will inevitably mean ruthlesssly pruning their existing schedules, in particular cutting out a surfeit of Christian meetings and making room for genuine friendships with those without Christ. In a home church Christians can specifically help one another to plan their lives accordingly.

## Patient cultivation

The second priority for effective reaping of the harvest is patient cultivation both of those to be mobilised for evangelism and those to be evangelised. We all know of horror-stories about insensitive, gauche and theologically inaccurate proselytes; but that should not justify any wet blanket technique in dampening the ardour, especially of those newly converted, whose experience of Jesus is clear, contagious and uncomplicated. The sad thing is when more mature, knowledgeable Christians lose the fire in their belly and actually stop evangelising. The home church can fan the flames and direct them wisely.

In fact, the ongoing — and hopefully maturing — life of the home church will strengthen and refresh the witnessing of its members. As Christians grow in their experience of Jesus, they have more to share in presenting him to others. In the often-quoted report of the Church of England over thirty years ago entitled: 'Towards the Conversion of England,' the following recommendation was made:

'. . . That in every congregation there should be found groups or cells of people who have the concern for evangelism deeply at heart, and are prepared to give time and effort to it. . . . And that these groups should be composed of those who desire, by habits of personal devotion, by study, by planning together, by pooling experience, to equip themselves for ordinary, everyday witness to Christ in their neighbourhood, at their work, and in their leisure.'

If each home church followed through these four methods of cultivating its members for evangelism, the face of the church as a whole would gradually be changed, and there would be labourers in the ripe fields reaping the harvest. Jesus spent three full years patiently cultivating his workers. He trained them on the job. He showed them by his own example. He put them to work, supervising them on occasions, but on others sending them out in pairs to learn as they did it. He spent time de-briefing them and taught them as much by their mistakes as by their successes. He expected them to reproduce by witnessing to him as Lord and King; when Peter publicly confessed Jesus as the Christ, he asserted: 'On this rock I will build my church, and the gates of hell shall not be able to withstand it.'

As Christians thus witness to Jesus, the church is established, grows and breaks the stranglehold of Satan. 'His whole evangelistic strategy — indeed, the fulfilment of his very purpose in coming into the world, dying on the cross, and rising from the grave — depended on the faithfulness of his chosen disciples to this task. It did not matter how small the group was to start with, so long as they reproduced and taught their disciples to reproduce. This was the way his church was to win — through the dedicated lives of those who knew the Saviour so well that his Spirit and method constrained them to tell others. As simple as it may seem, this was the way the gospel would conquer. He had no other plan.'[10]

In summarising the evangelistic strategy of Jesus, Robert Coleman urges that we follow the same route — begin with a few people; stay together as a unit so that each can interact in love and trust with the others; do as many things together as possible; arrange specific times when the group meets to study the Bible, share burdens and deepest desires, and to pray; build up opportunities for sharing the gospel which really stretch each person; do not let anyone get isolated, either in their witnessing or in their burdens, but make sure there is proper supervision, encouragement and freedom to operate; and above all see to it that each one is daily being filled with the Spirit to live for Christ.[11] If home churches are really operating as they should, this will be the outcome.

If the evangelists need to be cultivated, so do those to be evangelised. Of course, it is very easy to slip into an attitude which sees human beings as having souls to be saved, and making friends as a means to this end. That looks — and often feels — like manipulation and headcounting. We cultivate the unconverted only by loving them without strings, loving them with the love of the Lord, loving them because he has first loved us. In fact, the love we are to have for unbelievers is no different from the love we are to have for one another in the body of Christ. We saw in Chapter 2 that Jesus did not have any greater love for his disciples than for the crowds, even though he was able to show it more fully to those who chose to share their lives with him. We are called to share our lives and our love with unbelievers in the same way.

This love will show itself in sitting where they sit, sharing in their interests, hurting when they hurt. If evangelism is sharing the good news of Jesus, it will naturally spill over from this identification. Evangelism is not, therefore, something we really decide we will do when the opportunity presents itself, let alone because that is the thing Christians are meant to do and I must do my bit. Evangelism is the natural overflow of knowing Jesus the Lord and walking in the Spirit. What comes out when people bump into us indicates the state of our inner hearts — 'from the abundance of the heart the mouth speaks' . . . 'We cannot but speak of what we have seen and heard.'[12]

## Flexible methods

Costas' third priority is flexibility of space and methods. We are concerned particularly for the distinctive ways in which a home church can operate evangelistically. Here we need to stress the converting power of the meeting itself. Most of those who came to know Christ through the ministry of John Wesley, however much their hearts were awakened to spiritual truth through hearing him preach, actually experienced the reality of conversion in the class meetings.[13] The situation in Seoul speaks for itself: Yonggi Cho's strategy is for each cell member, and particularly the leader, to invite neighbours in any need to the home cell meeting. He relates one incident at length:

'A woman from our congregation witnessed to a woman she had met at the neighbourhood supermarket. She had overheard the woman, an unbeliever, telling a friend about problems with her marriage. She was on the verge of divorce. It turned out that our member had had some very similar problems, but the Lord Jesus had saved her marriage through prayer and through the ministry of the home fellowship.

'Outside the market our member caught up with the other woman and said, 'I couldn't help overhearing you discussing your problem with your friend. I had a very similar problem. Would you like to come over for tea while I tell you how I overcame that problem and saved my marriage?'

'To her surprise, the woman accepted on the spot. During the time of sharing, our member told how she and her husband had been at the point of almost agreeing to a divorce, when they met the Lord and their lives were turned around. She did not immediately urge the woman to accept Christ as her Saviour, but she did relate how much the home cell group meetings meant and invited the woman to the next one. She assured her that there were a lot of understanding women in the group, who would be able to identify with this woman's problems.

'When she attended the cell meeting for the first time, the woman was immediately impressed. Although she did have a little difficulty with the enthusiastic singing, the hand-clapping and so on, she saw that the women were all much like she was. Yet there was a serenity about them that she longed to have. She did not give her heart to Jesus that first meeting, but she was drawn back. Then a few meetings later she surrendered her life to the Lord, and she soon joined the church. Not long afterward her husband began to come to church too. Eventually he met the Lord, and the marriage was saved.'[14]

This story illustrates the value both of the home church and of the local church. The converting power of the body of Christ at worship, whether in the intimate atmosphere of a home or in the inspiring context of a larger congregation, should never be underestimated. Very frequently unbelievers are opened up to the Lord in the worship of the congregation: it does not really matter if and on what basis they make a public response at such a service — what does matter is that they are then grafted into a small group where they can continue to meet the Lord and reach a considered and deliberate commitment to Jesus as Lord.

In Oxford, we have Beginners' groups which function in precisely this way. From whatever direction people may have travelled — whether by personal conversation with a Christian friend, or dropping into a service which is impregnated with the presence of the Lord, or being gradually peppered with God's Word through regular exposure Sunday by Sunday, or in response to a specific invitation to turn to Christ — all are encouraged into such a group, meeting in someone's home, where the essence of Christian discipleship is explained and shared. There may be 16–20 people with four sharing the leadership. Each meeting combines a session altogether with breaking down into groups of four or five. At the first meeting, each person shares how they happen to be present at such a meeting, and it becomes obvious that people have come in varied states of spiritual dress and undress. It is rare that the course ends without all having made a clear commitment to Jesus.

A very similar pattern has been established in a remote diocese of Brazil by the local grassroots communities. A situation more different from central Oxford would be difficult to imagine — the area is on the western rim of the Amazon jungle close to the Bolivian border. Rubber-tapping and Brazil-nut gathering have been replaced by a lumber industry and by large cattle ranches. The basic needs of peasants and aborigines can no longer be met adequately from the now–ravaged environment, and the large-estate owners care for little except their own interests. Here, each grassroots community is made up of 'evangelistic groups', which function as grassroots cells for the specific purpose of evangelisation. They meet once or twice a week for singing, spontaneous prayer, and introducing visitors and new members. They also review each member's problems and achievements, and discuss possible solutions. A passage of Scripture is read and commented upon — in the Good News Bible, which has been subsidised by the diocese and distributed to virtually every member of the many grassroots communities in the area. A typical meeting will close with spontaneous prayer, followed by the Lord's Prayer.[15]

A group of home churches in the same area — perhaps three or four — could between them provide the personnel for such Beginners' or Enquirers' groups to welcome and teach those interested in the gospel as a result of the witnessing life of their members. Where such witnessing is being consistently maintained, such groups would become an almost continuous feature of the local congregation's life.

There are, of course, numerous ways in which evangelism can be carried on in a local church or in home churches, but this is not the place to itemise them. Each locality will have methods which suit its character. The gifts within a home church will usually indicate the kind of evangelism which will reflect its life, whether through music or cooking or handicrafts or drama etc.

## Open homes

Two methods, however, need to be clearly mentioned, because they are often so obvious that they are missed or even dismissed. These are open homes and open-air preaching. A fascinating little fact is that the Greek word translated 'hospitality' in the New Testament literally means 'love for strangers': *philoxenia*.[16] 'Strangers' in the New Testament refers primarily to those outside the kindom of God, or to those outside the normal limits of society, or to those whom we have never met. We are to show practical love for them, especially by opening our homes to them. Indeed, such love for strangers became so integrally bound up with making homes available, that the word came to mean 'hospitality'.

To a very significant degree the ministry of Jesus depended on the availability of homes. There are many incidents in the gospels where he was invited into a home.[17] In homes he taught, healed, forgave sins, liberated, worshipped, wept, prayed. In the so-called parable of the sheep and the goats, he said: 'I was a stranger and you took me in.'[18] Love always implies hospitality, both for Jesus and for his apostles. Paul talks of love, brotherly affection, contributing to the needs of Christians and hospitality in the same breath.[19] Peter enjoins hospitality without any murmuring (the word here echoes the murmuring of the children of Israel in the wilderness[20], because such practical love 'covers a multitude of sins'[21] — he obviously knew something of the strains imposed on willing hosts and hostesses (particularly hostesses) by the biblical injunction. '*Philoxenia* is to be shown to all. It is striking that Paul puts it between duties to the saints and one's persecutors (an expression of love which Polycarp, bishop of Smyrna, extend to his persecutors[22]). In Christ all barriers are removed. . . . In times of persecution, hospitality to refugees and exiles was most important. But in times of peace, too, the hospitality of fellow-believers was often claimed in that travel-loving age. . . . Hospitality is seen as a divine *charisma* of believers, a gift of His Spirit. . . . There may be angelic visitations as a result.'[23]

The Christian home, therefore, is one major focus of all ministry in the name of the Lord, but particularly of evangelism. An extra place at the table for someone living on their own or a rejected teenager will provide unique opportunities for sharing the love of Christ. Special open evenings, with a speaker talking clearly about Christ, will play their part. The spare bedrom, offering shelter and space to a beleaguered mother or an estranged husband, can become the place of encounter with Christ.

## Open-air preaching

Open-air preaching was equally fundamental to the ministry of Jesus. When he is not recorded as ministering in homes, or teaching in the local synogogues or in the temple, he is proclaiming the gospel of the kingdom in the open air. Of course, the climate was far more conducive than that of northern Europe, but that should not have stopped us using this method of evangelism far more widely. In terms of spiritual impact on the forces of darkness, against whom our real struggle is directed,[24] it is a totally different matter proclaiming the lordship of Jesus in the open air from preaching in a church. The one context challenges the prince of this world; the other essentially encourages the faithful believers.

One of the countries where the gospel is making special headway today is Chile. The spiritual atmosphere is, almost uniquely, very clear and free, according to many local Christians with experience elsewhere. They reckon that this open atmosphere is due to several decades of steady open-air preaching by Pentecostal Christians. The grip of Satan on the country has been broken by such boldness, and thousands are now turning to Christ. Whenever there has been a tide of spiritual revival, an essential element has always been open-air preaching. It began with Jesus himself, was spectacularly illustrated on the day of Pentecost and on other occasions in Jerusalem, was the hallmark of Paul's ministry, and has broken out on several occasions in the history of the church —

not least in England through the preaching of John Wesley and George Whitefield. Wesley wrote in his journal on Saturday, March 31, 1739:

'In the evening I reached Bristol and met Mr. Whitefield there. I could scarce reconcile myself at first to this strange way of preaching in the fields, of which he set me an example on Sunday; having been all my life (until lately) so tenacious of every point relating to decency and order, that I should have thought the saving of souls almost a sin if it had not been done in a church. . . . At four in the afternoon (on the Monday next) I submitted to be more vile, and proclaimed in the highways the glad tidings of salvation, speaking from a little eminence in a ground adjoining to the city, to about three thousand people. The scripture on which I spoke was this, 'The Spirit of the Lord is upon me, because he has anointed me to preach the gospel to the poor!'

Wesley put many of his Christians to work as open-air preachers, and used his classes as Beginners' groups for any who were curious enough to take it further. Such 'field-preaching' today — in shopping precincts, sportsgrounds, street corners, stations, airports, pubs, school playgrounds etc. — if backed up by different audio-visual aids like singing, sketching, street theatre or dance, would provide many opportunities for getting out amongst the ordinary people. If this is done prayerfully and with careful planning, members of home churches can mingle with the crowds with the specific intention of drawing people into their fellowship. It is important to have such a goal and to pray accordingly, not to see the open-air work as an end in itself.

## Sensitivity to the Spirit

The fourth element in Costas' plan for effective harvesting is sensitivity and sacrificial dedication to the Spirit's movement in people's lives — so that we know when to speak and when to keep silent, when to invite and when to visit, when to pursue and when to leave well alone. Only the love of God can be a reliable guide at this point. Knowing when and how to press people to a point of decision to commit their lives to

Christ is an essential facet of what makes the ministry of an evangelist.

The last word on the theme of evangelism must be spoken from Latin America, not least because we began this chapter with a reminder of the current search for integrity and wholeness in mission as a whole:

'A community is Christian because it evangelises: this is its task, its reason for being, its life. Evangelising is a diverse and complex action; a Christian community is called upon to evangelise in all that it does: by words and by works. To evangelise is to announce the true God, the God revealed in Christ: the God who covenanted with the oppressed and their cause, the God who frees his people from injustice, from oppression and from sin.'[25]

CHAPTER 9

# A friend's birthday

*'People should look upon the happenings of everyday life as faith-events. The things that happen ought to be celebrated in faith — a good harvest, a friend's birthday, the companionship of one's workmates, rejoicing over the local team's victory, the cooperation involved in helping to build a house for a neighbour, and so on. . . . Every event in our lives is a sacrament, if it serves to bring us nearer to God and to men. . . .'*

The exciting vista spread before a home church is the realistic possibility of genuinely sharing the whole of daily life as a Christian family. 'Everything created by God is good, and nothing is to be rejected, if it is received with thanksgiving; for then it is consecrated by the word of God and prayer.'[1] Inevitably, so much local church life is superficial and fragmentary. The size and the structures necessitate that. The benefits of meeting in a larger congregation can be appreciated without niggle, if we are each part of a home church where we can be ourselves and share ourselves with others. There is so much to celebrate and, certainly in Northern Europe, we need to learn how to celebrate. We make such an effort and a chore out of virtually everything, including worship. Other cultures have so much to teach us about celebration.

This is very plain in Latin America, where a fiesta is celebrated at the slightest provocation. It was an education to be in Costa Rica immediately before Christmas: while most people in Britain find the Christmas preparations a grind, the people of San Jose were manifestly enjoying themselves. Whole families walk through the streets of the city, thronging the thoroughfares, as they do the shopping and simply enjoy being alive. Yes, it is warm and the evenings are balmy — but there is not nearly so much to go around, nor is there such a wealth of goods in the shops. One of the most exhilarating experiences I have ever had was to be part of a massive crowd of at last 150,000 in the vast Maracana soccer stadium in Rio de Janeiro, watching a fiery, but skilful, match between the leading Rio teams — Flamenco and Fluminense. Passions ran high, but there was none of the ugliness of English soccer crowds. The occasion was a fiesta — drums, fire crackers, maraccas, the lot. The same is true on the religious festivals and, however much one aims off for superstitions and nominal elements, these are times of high drama and colour.

The same is true in Africa. It is almost beyond belief how blacks in South Africa, especially Christians, manage to celebrate life in any way, such is the daily dehumanisation and oppression to which the *apartheid* system subjects them. But be given the privilege of joining in a special celebration at Easter or when the bishop visits the parish or on their patronal festival, and you will experience a new dimension of exuberant joy at being alive as a child of God.

## A fiesta or a chore?

No doubt it is true that such celebration in Africa and Latin America is partly due to the sense of relief with which the poor can bring a little colour and carnival to a drab existence. But that is not the whole story: celebration does not come easily to those brought up on the Protestant work ethic, and a niggardly attitude to anything that looks extravagant can easily dominate the proceedings. When we do let our hair down, there tends to be an atmosphere of suspended guilt, as if we shouldn't really be doing it and anyway there's a huge bill to pay at the end.

Now it is obviously wrong to take on board another cultural approach without checking it out biblically. When it comes to celebration, it is clear that the Bible is full of it. Especially in the world of the Old Testament there is an unrestrained, full-blooded *joie de vivre* which permeates the worship of God's people at the best of times. Many of the Psalms are full of this exuberant joy. It spills over into the worship of the early church: the English version of Acts 2:46 (which is describing the first home-church situation) betrays the Anglo-Saxon restraint of the translators — 'Day by day, attending the temple together and breaking bread from home to home, they partook of food with glad and generous hearts.' The word translated 'glad' actually means 'full of exultation'. In Heb. 1:9 it is used in connection with oil, referring to the oil with which people anointed themselves at festivals (fiestas).[2] It has the sense of being overjoyed with the delights of being called into the fellowship of God's people, an unrestrained pride (in the right sense, of course) in having been made a child of God. In the Greek translation of the Old Testament (the Septuagint) 'the meaning of the word is the cultic joy which celebrates and extols the help and the acts of God.'[3] Heaven and earth, mountains and islands are summoned to take part in the celebration. In the book of Revelation it is at the heart of the joy of heaven:[4] When the glory of the Lord Jesus is fully revealed, we will then rejoice 'with joy unspeakable and full of glory.'[5] This sense of being a community which anticipates that great wedding-feast of the Lamb throbs at the heart of the worship of God's people in the New Testament. 'Glad' is hardly the word to describe that!

We have looked at this word in its widest connotations, because it enshrines the essence of true worship. In the Western church we have managed to separate sacred and secular, divine and human, worship and daily life, to the extent that we are awkward with any sacramental approach to the reality of the world around us. In the Bible, worship is the whole person presenting to God in thanksgiving and adoration the whole of his experience and the whole of his world. Paul makes this clear in his classic exhortation: 'I appeal to you brethren, by the mercies of God, to present your bodies as a living sacrifice, holy and acceptable to God, which is your spiritual worship.'[6] Thanksgiving for all that God has done for us in Christ, i.e. gratitude for grace upon grace, is the dominant characteristic of the new man, which Paul perceives to be the community of the Holy Spirit,[7] not an individualistic phenomenon. Gratitude and grace have the same Greek root — *charis* = grace, *eucharistia* = thanksgiving. The Christian life is, fundamentally and pervasively, a eucharistic community-experience. Breaking bread together, a daily fact of life, has

become a sacrament of all that God has done for us in Jesus —
and it it, therefore, quite natural for Christians to celebrate
the eucharist together frequently. That action expresses (in
community) the heart of the gospel. This becomes invested
with a particular dimension of joy unspeakable when it is
consciously rooted in the certainty of Christ's return in glory,
and more particularly in the heavenly banquet of which our
eucharistic meals on earth are a foretaste.[8]

The earliest home churches in Jerusalem followed this
pattern and rhythm of life. They were a celebrating community, and they were not ashamed to show it. We are heirs of the
same fiesta tradition, and in our own home churches we can
explore what it will mean for us today.

## The Eucharist in the home

One implication has to be faced fairly and squarely from the
outset, namely the freedom of home churches to celebrate the
eucharist without restraint. In view of the Catholic doctrine of
the Mass, it is nothing short of remarkable that grassroots
communities in various Latin American countries are pressing
ahead with this essential activity of the church. Normally the
bread and the wine are consecrated by the priest in the local
church building, taken to the homes of the people, and then
distributed to all. Most of the time the priest is not present,
and any lay man or woman will preside. Sometimes the same
procedure (using the 'reserved' sacrament) takes place, even
when the priest is present. This is not the place to argue the
biblical basis of the priesthood of all believers, and its
implications for eucharistic celebration in home churches.
The procedure just described, which is not confined to Roman
Catholics, has absolutely no theological basis; in fact, the
whole movement in these grassroots communities highlights
the alien nature of such a sacerdotal preserve at the heart of
their life. The whole movement is as thorough a demonstration of the priesthood of all believers as one can find anywhere
in the world, including the Protestant churches who claim to
base their doctrine and life on that article of faith.

As we might expect, there is no shortage of Catholic
commentators who are putting the crucial question, directly

or indirectly, to the hierarchy. For example, Jose Marins expressed this hope, when asked about what he wanted to see happen in Latin America and elsewhere:
'I hope that life will not be obstructed in the name of the structure. I'd wish to mention here the longing for new ministries, so that the communities may have the possibility of celebrating the Eucharist. Perhaps this will be a reality in the next century! I hope that the centre of our Church progressively recognizes the life which these communities experience and express and, through a change in the pastoral discipline, help them to reach maturity, to become eucharistic communities amidst the people.'[9]

In the San Paulo Community in Rome in 1973 a fascinating situation emerged when the senior priest (an Abbot) was forced to resign, because he was bucking the system too radically. The community was compelled to meet for worship in a nearby warehouse. Almost immediately several quesions of a practical nature, but overhung with profound theological considerations, began to surface:

*Baptism* 'Should baptism take place in the real community to which the people belonged — or should they go to some other church which would provide more adequate ecclesiastical status? What is baptism in any case? Is it largely ceremonial? What weight has baptism in the whole Christian understanding of life?'

*Eucharist.* 'The Abbot was debarred from presiding at the Mass. . . . Other priests could preside. But what if, in turn, they were all debarred? Would it be proper for this Christian community, in an orderly way, to appoint lay people to preside? What is this sacrament? Why is so much made of it? Who has the right to celebrate? Is it a people's act or a priestly act?'

*Marriage.* 'At some point, in the middle of the Mass, a young man and a young woman stepped forward and said something like this: 'We ask you, members of this Christian community, before God and in the middle of this Mass, to accept us as husband and wife from this day forward. Before you, we take one another for better, for worse; for richer, for poorer; in sickness and in health; to love and to cherish, till death do us part.' What should be done? Is marriage a sacrament, and if it is, what does that mean? What makes a marriage, essentially? What is the part of priest, couple, congregation?'[10]

## Celebration as a lifestyle

Putting on one side the many subsidiary questions which are relevant only to Roman Catholics, and ignoring the apparent fact in the Rome community that it actually seemed to have existed over against the local church, not as a microcosm of it, these examples give us important clues about the way home churches can develop a lifestyle which truly covers the whole of life — and in a celebratory context. If they are to *be* the church, is there anything traditionally or (more important) biblically expected of the local congregation which cannot legitimately be expected to emerge in their growing life together? Will not many things, especially those relating more personally to individual members, be much better expressed there?

In one Brazilian parish, where the grassroots communities have come to express the whole life of the congregation, only the children of parents who are members of the communities or who have godparents similarly committed can be baptized. The catechesis of children is done in the communities, and the priest conducts marriages only after consultation with the leadership of the communities.[11] This way seems to have a strongly disciplinary ring about it, but it shows how every aspect of a Christian's life can be embraced within a home church.

Another example from Brazil comes from a grassroots community in Rio de Janeiro:

'This community consists of about 20 families. . . . Each Sunday morning they meet to celebrate the Word — that is, read the Gospel passage, reflect on it, sing hymns and pray. The day I was there, one of the couples was celebrating 25 years of marriage. On a special occasion like this they have a eucharist. The whole celebration was joyful, informal and very spiritual. Lasting about two hours, it included a good hour's discussion about marriage. People shared experiences, both good and bad, and began to analyse the causes of marriage problems — people forced to work long hours for low pay, the struggle for decent housing, the impossible costs of doctors and medicines. The priest ... very gently deepened the discussion. ... I cannot describe the joy, seriousness and spirituality of that eucharist. ... Members of this grassroots community are a dynamic force in the neighbourhood. They really are the leaven — through discussing neighbourhood problems and the gospel together, people experience a clear call to action.'[12]

In the past the Roman Catholic Church has used the Mass as a means of maintaining its control over its people. In the grassroots communities, the Eucharist is 'both a magnet that draws the community together for spiritual strength, and a dynamo that energises the people of God and spins them out into the world in service and in witness.'[13]

It is exceedingly important to see worship as embracing the whole of life, and to discover relevant, practical ways in which the whole of life can be expressed in specific acts of worship. There are many practical hints which would enhance, in one way, the worshipping life of a home church. But these become techniques, not living components, if the members are not learning more and more to see and to celebrate the grace of God in everything that happens. When every aspect of our lives can be celebrated in true worship, it becomes natural to express the presence of God to others in the midst of what is happening. Thus, mission and evangelism flow out of worship. Indeed the two flow into each other: 'liturgy without mission is like a river without a spring: mission without worship is like a river without a sea. ... Put in other terms, the test of a vigorous worship experience will be a dynamic participation in mission. The test of a faithful involvement in mission will be a profound worship experience.'[14]

## A worshipping life

If, at its most profound, worship is presenting our bodies to the Lord as a living sacrifice (Romans 12:1), then the worship of the home church is an expression of the life which its members already share. Therefore, when the home church gathers, those in oversight, esp. the helmsman, need so to have their finger on its pulse that they are aware of the present condition of its health. They will then be able in a meaningful way to direct attention to God's character and perfection. One week the stress will fall on repentance and confession, the next on thanksgiving. Adoration, which lifts such worship from ordinariness, will hopefully run like a golden thread through all the life of a home church.

From this it is plain that the worship of a home church is not just a slot at the beginning or the end, or indeed at any point during its time together. We cannot say on any one week 'Right, we'll start with worship'. Worship is a way of life and the life of the home church should be a worshipping life — explicitly when it gathers. The presence of God in the midst is acknowledged throughout the time together, and the character of this very present God will be continually under consideration in relation to everything that happens.

Furthermore, a great responsibility falls on all members to prepare themselves for the meeting of the home church. Those with oversight particularly need to spend good time together, sensitizing themselves to the presence and character of God as well as to the current condition of the home church. It is necessary to pave the way in developing what can be called 'skills of worship'. The better the preparation and the more 'tools' at people's disposal, the more free they will be to respond to the promptings of the Spirit. It is important to see 'psalms, hymns and spiritual songs' as tools. Too frequently, singing becomes the beginning and end of worship. There is a crucial need for guidance in what it means to listen to God's Spirit, as the home church gathers in the conscious presence of God. Songs and hymns learned by heart become vehicles for praise and adoration.

Silence is a powerful tool for shedding the cares and failures of the day — guided silence, gently but firmly maintained. Certain cultures are so frenetic in their sheer pace of life, that deliberately 'cooling it' is essential to worship and to listening to God. Worship should also be seen as part of the mutual ministry of the home church members one to another. Without too much justification, worship has been seen exclusively in a vertical context. Sensitivity to one another in the home church at worship is a ministry which truly builds up the body

of Christ. This is true not simply in the area of particular ways
of expressing praise and adoration (e.g. with uplifted hands,
clapping, praying out loud in a tongue by and for oneself). It
is valuable also, for example, in singing. A strong voice needs
to be restrained and the emphasis place on personal harmony
between members expressed in musical harmony.

As with every part of the life of a home church, the enabling
ministry of those with oversight is vital — encouraging anyone
to take the lead when thus guided by the Sprit — whether in
spoken prayer, or beginning a song, or reading a Scripture, or
suggesting that a particular direction or theme or activity be
adopted at any given time. This freedom to give sensitive
leadership is integral to pastoral care. Much ministry will be
released to the members by such leadership.

## Sensitive leadership

There are few things more refreshing and encouraging to a
home church than to discover the ways God leads worship in
unforeseen and unplanned ways. Under sensitive leadership
each person responds out of his resources (including those
'tools' and skills previously mentioned) to the promptings of
the Holy Spirit. Needs are met, wounds are healed, sins are
uncovered, burdens are lifted — without there necessarily
being any explicit ministry.

A key passage, which brings together the theme of celebrating the whole of life and the reality of worship together is
Hebrews 12:28, 29, 13: 14–16. In this part of Hebrews,
worship is seen as both service and sacrifice. Because we are
reluctant to be servants and because we are not prepared for
the sacrifice involved in truly 'acceptable worship' (12:28), it
is rare for us to experience worship that is a foretaste of
heaven.

A closer look at 13:15 will give us an important clue:
'Through Jesus let us continually offer up a sacrifice of praise
to God, that is, the fruit of lips that acknowledge His Name.'
Lips that acknowledge the Name of Jesus hold the key to
acceptable worship. We have sadly reduced confessing Jesus
as Lord (because 'Lord' is the Name which is above every
name) to 'giving your testimony' in a church building. When

the New Testament talks of bearing testimony and acknowledging the Name of the Lord, it is thinking of the market-
place, the godless world of our daily living. Acceptable
worship, says the writer, is 'the fruit' of acknowledging Jesus
as Lord before the world — i.e. the natural outgrowth of a
consistent life of daily witness to the kingship of Jesus.

When a home church, or a local congregation, gathers out
of that kind of daily living, it will discover the reality of
acceptable worship. We cannot drum this up amongst people
whose bodies are not presented to God all through the week.
The little phrase in 13:15 translated 'continually' literally
means 'through everything'— i.e. worship is either a lifestyle
or it is non-existent. It certainly involves sacrifice, saying 'No'
to ourselves and 'yes' to God.

Such worship, when God's people gather to give praise to
God, has two inner dynamics, one activating and the other
controlling. Cf. 12:28, where the little word 'thus' refers to the
gratitude mentioned at the beginning of the verse. Worship is
fired by gratitude. The root word here is *charis*, or grace, and
the heart of our gratitude is the grace of God in Jesus — what
Paul calls (in Rom. 12:1) 'the mercies of God', which he has
expounded in Chapters 1–11 and now makes the basis of his
appeal for presenting our bodies to God as a living sacrifice.
We have received an unshakeable kingdom: 'Jesus Christ is
the same, yesterday, today and for ever'[15] — let that inspire
our worship.

### Reverence and awe

If gratitude activates acceptable worship, then it is controlled
by 'reverence and awe'. It is a pity that these words have
become equated with what is drab, dour and even dead. They
do not denote solemnity so much as a sense of being answerable to God for our worship. Jesus warned us that we would
have to render account for 'every careless word',[16] and we are
all guilty of careless words when we take part in corporate
worship, whether we are liturgically orientated or not.

Reverence and awe are frequently experienced through
silence, and evangelicals particularly need to learn to worship
the Lord in the beauty of holy silence. 'When the Lamb

opened the seventh seal, there was silence in heaven for about half an hour,'[17] and if worship is the life of heaven, then silence is an essential part of its praise. We need to be awed into silence by the presence of the Lord in our midst.

Another part of reverent awe is the involvement of our whole being in worship.[18] Paul urged us to present our BODIES to God, and there is no reason why this should be suspended in worship. For historical and sociological reasons, not for any good biblical ones, we have often allowed dance and drama, colour and variety to be squeezed out of the worshipping community. Westerners have also a fear of total worship — the mind is in strict control, and we are frightened of what the Scriptures call our *splagchna*, or guts. Worship which includes, and even emanates from, our guts is by no means inferior. If we were more honest, it is this superior attitude which makes it difficult for those conditioned by Western values even to think of mixing freely with those from other cultures as a worshipping community.

We have also allowed the clock to dictate to us. If true and acceptable worship is the essential activity of eternity, then (by definition) we lose sense of time. We know we have begun to worship the Lord, when we no longer look at our watches. Here 'African time' has so much to teach us. It is a bare fact of experience that, when we truly lose ourselves, three hours passes like a flash.

Another crippling drawback to acceptable worship is the very architecture of our church buildings. Long, narrow, high buildings, filled with pews are a contradiction of all the Scriptures teach about the church as a worshipping community. And, strange to relate, it is the most 'de-priested' denominations who normally invest in priestly buildings, with the pulpit (rather than the altar) several feet above the people, rooted foursquare in the middle at the front. There the minister (who is definitely *not* a 'priest') stands and the people have to look at him throughout the 'service of worship' — or close their eyes. 'Where two or three are gathered together in My Name, there am I in the midst,' said Jesus. Most church buildings do not encourage that reality — home churches do.

Yes, home churches give an ideal context for turning the whole of life into a sacrament of God's grace and truth in Jesus.

# CHAPTER 10

# The chauffeur and the steering wheel

*'To think of a Christian who doesn't want to serve is like thinking of a chauffeur who doesn't know how to keep hold of the steering wheel. So the church ought to serve, and to free, those who need its love most.'*

Chauffeurs drive cars: that is their function. Christians serve others: that is their function. A Christian who is not serving is as much an anomaly as a chauffeur who cannot drive the car. Our model, as always, is Jesus, who came 'not to be served, but to serve, and to give his life a ransom for many.'[1] If we want basic assurance of our position in Jesus Christ, this is our pointer: 'By this we may be sure that we are in him, he who says he abides in him ought to walk in the same way in which he walked.'[2]

This servant spirit is so alien to our nature that we constantly need to check out whether we are living in the way Jesus lived. This is particularly necessary for larger congregations which, in experiencing the blessing of God, can become not simply large but presumptuous, paternalistic and triumphalist. One of the noticeable qualities of the spiritually-sensitive Christian who is a loyal member of such a congregation is a sense of dis-ease and godly discontent, particularly when any traces of complacency reveal themselves in the life of the church. It is very important for its leaders to listen very carefully to such feelings expressed by ordinary people. It is tempting to treat such douches of cold water as marks of disloyalty, pessimism or troublemaking. They are far more likely to be God-given prods to the conscience, to prevent a blind slide into the Laodicean sickness.[3]

## Detecting the signs of pride

A network of home churches, with properly oiled channels of communication into the centre, is an excellent way of reinforcing a spirit of service after the model of Jesus. This commitment to *diakonia* is best captured and expressed where a few people know one another well enough to hit the first signs of pride and domination of others. It will be valuable, therefore, to ask ourselves leading questions about the corporate life in which we are involved — not just once, but regularly. In the same way as home churches need to brainstorm about evangelism, so they need to examine their life together in terms of service.

The kind of questions we need to ask are these. In what ways is our home/local church really serving the local church, or is it an independent unit looking after its own life? Are we actually making ourselves available to specific individuals, in order to minister to their needs? Is our motive self-fulfilment or a desire to help others? In what ways are we denying ourselves rights and pleasures in order to be at the disposal of others? Is our service given from a position of seemingly unselfish availability, or are we subtly using this role to keep others under our control — i.e. are we using Christian service as a means of manipulating or controlling others? Is the service we give a platform for our talents or a joyful celebration of our debt to Jesus? Are we falling into the temptation of totting up our acts of service to bolster our reputation before others or even our standing before God? Do we see our gifts and ministry as truly given by God, consecrated to God, available for God, dispensable by God, and instruments for God's glory?

## Power under control

Any talk of '*my* church, *my* gifts, *my* ministry' can actually indicate a spirit of domination, not service. Perhaps the only effective way of evaluating our Christian service is to examine briefly the way Jesus walked, so that we are reminded of what being a servant meant for him. Although he did not cling on to equality with God, but made himself of no reputation, humbling himself and became an obedient servant, Jesus was invested (in his earthly life) with the power of the Spirit. That power was strictly under control, and he used it to meet the needs of all kinds of people, not to further his own ends or reputation.

A swift reading of Mark's gospel gives us a kaleidoscope of his service in the power of the Spirit — he ministered to the demonised, the sick, the leper, the paralysed, the tax-collectors, a man with a withered hand, the spiritually hungry and the physically hungry, a woman with haemorrhaging, a father desperate for his critically-ill daughter, the deaf and the dumb, the blind, the children, the Samaritans, the Gentiles. All the time he was serving his disciples as well, encouraging and exhorting, training and correcting, equipping and preparing.

He fuelled this ministry with regular, disciplined times of prayer, when he re-aligned himself with his Father's heart and will. Although he was not prepared to turn away from anyone or to turn anyone away from him, nevertheless Jesus obviously went out deliberately to those in need of a physician.[4] If, like Jairus[5] (the ruler of the local synagogue), top people came to him with a real need, he met them right where they were. If, like the rich young ruler,[6] they had no need except to get rid of surplus wealth, he made that the central issue of the encounter. Jesus was serving that young man by pinpointing his real need and, by implication, offering to meet it by inviting him to relinquish the false security of riches in favour of joining the community of his disciples in following him.

Jesus served his contemporaries by going unerringly for the point of their real needs. Sometimes these were obvious, although even then he would insist on the person facing up to and articulating that need ('What do you want me to do for you?'[7]). On other occasions, he would gradually but inexorably lay bare the fundamental, not the presented, need ('My son, your sins are forgiven'[8]). Not infrequently, he would arouse an awareness of need, hitherto unrecognized, by touching a person's strength ('Go, sell what you have and give to the poor'[9]). Having thus isolated the true needs of a person, Jesus offered himself as the one able to meet them, always leaving the summons to discipleship in his wake.

We are called to walk as he walked. By his Spirit we are enabled to walk as he walked. Hand in hand with our brothers and sisters we can walk as he walked. As individuals on our own we will be vulnerable in the extreme, the prey of our own gullibility or selfishness and the targets of exploiters and manipulators. Together we can discern true needs in people who seem adequate and self-sufficient; and together we can provide resources which are absolutely necessary if individuals are not to fold under pressure. In Chapter 13 we tackle the distinctive difficulties of developing a home church ministry in more affluent situations — at this stage, it simply needs saying that the needs of such people are often in the area of giving away rather than of receiving. The increasingly popular message that, if we put our trust in God, we will prosper physically and materially, is one thing when proclaimed to the poor and needy in terms of life's necessities; it is quite another thing when addressed to those who already have more than enough, turning their 'wants' into imagined 'needs'. We do not serve the affluent minority of the world by pushing them into greater and greater affluence.

### The needy and the marginalised

It is clear, therefore, that after the example of Jesus we should be seeking out the needy and the marginalised, while being sensitive and straight with those who cross our path who are not so clearly in need. Here it is right to say that, in the countries of Africa and Latin America, the needs of the underprivileged are blatant and overwhelming. For this reason it is impossible to walk as Jesus walked without serving others in their clamant, crushing needs. There can be no mission with integrity without such *diakonia*. Likewise, in South Africa, the servant-calling of the church has unmistakeable and inescapable application to the racial divisions of the country. Only the deliberately blind and the callously indifferent can deny that, let alone turn their backs on such a ministry of reconciliation.

But who are the needy and the marginalised in Europe and North America? Whom should the church, and in particular our home churches, be seeking out? Because the majority of

the people who cross our paths do not have such blatant
needs, in what direction should we deliberately move in order
'to seek and to save the lost'? Of course, the needy are not
exclusively the materially impoverished. The marginalised are
not only those in slums and hovels, but all whose background
or occupation pushes them to the margins of society. Zacchaeus was one such isolated and lost person, because he was
regarded, not merely as an exploiter of the people, but as a
traitor to the country.[10] His real needs, as perceived and met
by Jesus, were to give away much of his possessions and to
make restitution in many directions.

The 'holy eavesdropping' of Christians in Korea gives us a
way in to serving people where they are needy. For example,
the common incidence of divorce and marriage breakdown
if we are not careful, makes us insensitive to the trauma
involved in every single such family. Too often we allow
ourselves to be bemused and rendered impotent by the sheer
hugeness of the problem, when the Holy Spirit is perhaps
asking each home church to serve the needs of one aching
family. Most Christians are aware of the exhausting and
painful cost of ministering to people in such a situation. In a
home church, we can together care for both parents and the
children, maybe in small practical ways which echo the
menial foot-washing of Jesus. In the same way, single-parent
families are often deprived of the opportunity to be full and
accepted members of the community.

One particular community may marginalise different people from another community. A student-dominated area, and
church, can push the ordinary family to the margins of its life.
Usually the emphasis in a church attended by large numbers
of students is on the families providing hospitality for lonely
students. Very often, the students ought to be presented with
the privilege of serving the families. In another situation single
people can easily be marginalised, because the emphasis is so
much on family life. Great sensitivity is needed to avoid
driving a wedge between the unattached and families in a
local church; home churches have a special responsibility in
this area. In other, indeed in most, situations the elderly or
incapacitated are pushed off to the margins.

## Women and children

In many cultures, there is still a tendency to marginalise women and to highlight the men. In the *machismo* spirit of Latin America this is very marked, or indeed in certain parts or North America where worldly power is concentrated. The Spirit of Jesus urges Christian men to serve women, the norm being the way husbands are commanded to lay down their lives for their wives, in the same way as Christ loved the church, his bride, and gave himself for her.[11]

Before moving on to the more obviously needy in Western society, we need also to put question marks against the way we treat children. It goes without saying that they should be part and parcel of the life of home churches. This means a degree of imaginative flexibility and self-sacrifice on the side of the adults, so that children are included as welcome members, not merely tolerated and sent packing when they cause trouble on the principle that they should be seen and not heard. Genuinely to serve children in the Spirit of Jesus is a costly and demanding privilege. From different grassroots communities in Europe come these suggestive examples.

'Children belong to the whole development of the Community's life in a new way. . . . A statement of faith prepared by the congregation was led by a twelve-year old girl. . . . In a student church, children and their parents served communion. . . . Children have contributed substantially to the liturgy and are expected to participate in preparing it. . . . In community after community there is a habit, if something of significance has to be debated in a way which means that adults alone can be present, that the adults talk the matter over with the children for about two hours and bring the family mind, rather than simply an adult mind, as a contribution to the thinking.'[12]

This is a fulfilment of one important aspect of the kingdom of God: 'a little child shall lead them.' One of the most eloquently Christian traits in William Wilberforce[13] was his unalloyed pleasure in and respect for children, to whom he gave himself unstintingly in the midst of his immense political pressures and responsibilities, as well as his strategic initiatives in missionary and evangelistic ministry.

When we come to more obvious needs in Western society, it is again easy to produce a list which is so formidable that it immediately activates the switch-off mechanism built into all of us. Each home church should be asking the Lord to show them which person in what need he wants them to serve. If every such group up and down the country took on one such act of *diakonia*, the love of God would be transparently visible.

## Home church support

Alcoholics, drug addicts, down-and-outs, prostitutes, ex-prisoners (especially of the recidivist kind): these people have traditionally been the particular ministry of specialist Christian agencies or the unique calling of the Salvation Army. Many find their way to local churches, especially in the larger cities. They present a challenge and a problem to which there is no straightforward answer. Perhaps the way forward is by a joint ministry in cooperation between specialist agencies and home churches, organised through the local church or council of churches. What is clear is that such marginalised people need, perhaps more fundamentally than the more adequate, the closer support which a home church can provide. It is also clear that no one individual can carry the burden of supporting even one such person. In addition, the church can serve the wider community by making its human resources, such as a network of home churches, available to social welfare agencies in touch with these people.

There is a ministry of Christian support and service which home churches can give to unmarried mothers and to homosexuals. In recent years, they have not been so morally marginalised as in previous generations — for a number of reasons. Christians, in any case, should be involved in offering support and friendship, particularly when the cry for help goes up, however silently. Normally, the Christian attitude tends far more towards the statement of a moral position and, sometimes, entering into debate on such issues as abortion. Obviously, a Christian apologetic is essential, but biblically it needs to be fleshed out in loving action. If Christians in a home church feel strongly that ready access to abortion in unwanted pregnancies is wrong, then the complementary action is to give sympathetic support in practical ways to a mother-to-be. In the same way, if Christians take a biblical stance against practising homosexuality, the call of God comes to care for and to come alongside the neighbour who has homosexual tendencies.

Two particular groups of people are manifestly marginalised in most Western countries today — the unemployed and immigrants. Both situations call for a prophetic ministry to challenge and to change official attitudes, and for practical service to break down local barriers and to draw alongside in order to understand and help. I suppose nobody has any answer to unemployment, but the very least we can do is to welcome, listen and try to understand the unemployed as they touch, or indeed are found within, the life of our church. As far as the needs of immigrants are concerned, the dynamics of Christian compassion are, in effect, little different in liberal Western nations from those which operate in the enforced racial separation of South Africa. Specific and deliberate steps have to be taken to bring together in Christian fellowship (in the first instance) people from different cultural and racial backgrounds. A home church in one area can choose to meet with a home church in another area from time to time — if the two areas are ethnically distinct, as is usually the case.

## The acid test

In the set of examination questions posed earlier, we were asked to consider whether our particular home church in any sense serves the community of the local congregation. This often is the acid test of its servant-spirit. An independent-spirit so easily creeps into home groups, bringing a hyper-sensitivity and an introspectiveness that distance it from the rest of the body of Christ in that place. The ultimate result of this self-assertion is either separation or a slow death. There are many ways in which a home church can serve the body as a whole: it is worth giving a few examples.

In any congregation of some size, there is a constant need for those who will help to provide food and refreshments for central meetings. Often, literature needs to be distributed throughout the local community. Hard-worked secretaries need stamp-lickers, envelope-writers and paper-folders. Visitors need beds for the night — and longer: one American father-and-son came for one night and stayed three months, awaiting entry visas for Tanzania. People need lifts to church, to hospital, to friends and relatives. The main church services need welcomers, ushers, organisers and tidiers. The church grounds and buildings require dusters and polishers, sweepers and gardeners. These, and innumerable other, tasks are best done — not by the usual overworked few — but by each home church in rotation.

It is sad to see how unreliable Christians have become in such small things. We need a renewed spirit of *diakonia*, especially the ability to see that such service is the greatest we can offer in the kingdom of God.[14] The people chosen to 'serve tables' in the early church, in order to bring efficient help to widows (along with orphans a constantly-marginalised group in most societies), were men 'full of the Holy Spirit and wisdom.'[15] By their *diakonia* they released others, not just the widows, for their distinctive ministry.

# CHAPTER 11

# Yeast outside the dough

*'The church is the leaven of God's new world, the yeast put into the dough so that it will rise. A church remote from the world is like yeast outside the dough. In its own particular city, district, or place of work, each Christian community should be the leaven of this new world.'*

So far we have seen home churches which are small, personal and local; which are open to the Spirit's refreshing inspiration and variety; which combine mutual interdependence with individual distinctiveness; which are involved in mission and evangelism, celebration and service. Of one thing we can be certain: such home churches will attract, not merely interest, but opposition. They will certainly be like water to a thirsty land, but they will also be like lights in the darkness. More than that, they will find themselves impelled into action on behalf of those marginalised by society whom they have been led to love and to serve. That kind of action will provoke the anger and the resistance of those in power — both in the church and in the country.

## Collision with authority

This has always been so. Authentic testimony to Jesus the Lord has always brought the church into collision with authority. In glancing at the ministry of Jesus, we saw how he used open homes (both of friend and of foe), the open air, synagogues and the temple. What we did not explicitly underline is that he was invariably in conflict with the ecclesiastical and national hierarchy. The story of his life is one of escalating confrontation with the authorities. He did not go out to seek it; he inevitably attracted it — like moths drawn to the light, who seem to be attacking it but end up being singed by it.

This is obvious as we study any gospel account of his public ministry, culminating in his arrest, pseudo-trial and execution. It is graphically portrayed in all its ugliness in the actual narrative of the Passion. There, all the foci of power in the contemporary world united to wreak their vengeance on the one person in history who did not need power on earth, because he had supreme power through submission to his Father in heaven. His power was that of a servant, a suffering servant, a crucified servant, who won by being eliminated, who triumphed by being defeated. Those who work so hard to obtain and to maintain power in this world are fundamentally threatened by this kind of power. They can neither understand it nor explain it; it is alien to their world view and to their experience. When modern Pilates, Caiaphases, scribes and Pharisees encounter a recapitulation of the Christ-event in the witness of the church, they react in exactly the same way — stamp it out, get rid of it. There may be more or less sophisticated ways of doing it, but it will certainly be done.

It is important to register this certainty before we take a closer look at the prophetic ministry of the church as a whole, and therefore of the home church. Too many Christians have been thrown when steady faithfulness to Christ has met with such opposition, often because they had been taught to believe that things go better with Christ. It is also important to be aware of this inevitability of suffering and opposition in the harsh reality of what has frequently happened to leaders of grassroots communities in Latin America. Scores have been murdered by the death squads of some of the most repressive governments on earth. Countless others have been harassed, imprisoned, tortured, or have simply disappeared. Here is a story from Brazil:

'The small yellow-coloured object was carefully and almost reverently passed around the tight circle of people who had crowded into the clapboard shack of a Brazilian *favelado* (shanty-dweller). Several months before it had been smuggled out of a South American jail by members of the grassroots communities. The young priest, who had painstakingly carved his meagre soup-bone into the crude form of a dove, had sent it from his prison as a 'greeting' to thousands of grassroots communities in Latin America. His crime? He had dared to live out the consequences of his Christian faith as a coordinator of several small communities in one of the miserable shanty-towns that encircle the major cities of Latin America.'[1]

It is, of course, an easy matter to write and to read about such realities. It savours of guilt inducement on the one hand ('Why are we not suffering like that?'), and on the other of cheap scoring of points without being exposed to such risks ourselves ('You can't just talk about it'). What such stories can properly achieve is to challenge the comfortable in-group character of so much church life, particularly in home groups:

'In an age when the virtues of life-in-community are being extolled as an antidote to the anonymity of secular materialism, the grassroots communities have a special appeal. Yet they challenge our superficial and often narcissistic understanding of Christian community even more profoundly by their active involvement in the world around them. . . . They are also a challenge to our comfortable church life. . . . The majority, if not all, of the Protestant churches in Brazil have some kind of stake in maintaining the status quo. Rocking the boat is not an evangelical practice! We forget, however, that this is precisely what the early church, and many of its grassroots successors down through history, did: turn their sociocultural and political world upside down (cf. Acts 17: 1–9).'[2]

## Taking a stand

So we can expect opposition if we are being faithful to the mission and ministry of Jesus. It need not always result in unyielding resistance or persecution; sometimes there is opposition, but something is achieved by our stand for what is right. Recently in Brazil there was a national scandal over the bankruptcy of the social security system (allegedly because of official graft). Initially it was announced that the massive deficits would be made up out of the pay-packets of the workers. As a result of concerted pressure from every part of the country, particularly from the Catholic hierarchy speaking on behalf of strong support from the grassroots communities, the government eventually decided to withdraw their original solution and instituted new taxes, to come out of the pockets of the employers, to provide social security funds.[3]

In Cape Town in 1976, in the midst of a particularly wet and cold winter, the authorities decided to bulldoze a whole shanty-town, housing 20,000 people. The action was taken too suddenly to prevent it by protest, but many churches in the city decided to break three or four *apartheid*-inspired laws in order to provide temporary accommodation for some of these 'squatters' on church property. The parish of Wynberg erected about 25 tents to house over 100 people, also providing food, medical facilities and an advisory service. Such a response to human need in the face of unrighteousness was possible on that scale, because there was already in existence a network of home churches and of delegated leadership which could be used in such an emergency (in fact, the bulk of the ordained leadership was 1,000 miles away at a conference in Johannesburg at the time).

Both these examples show the possibility of united action, either on a national or a local scale, if there is an effective pattern of home churches in operation. Another imaginative example of such prophetic action comes from Recife in Brazil, where members of a grassroots community used street theatre to help 25,000 inhabitants of a local *favela* stand up to land speculators, who were attempting to evict them from their seaside shacks.[4]

## Action through mutual support

Wherever there has been authentic spiritual life rooted in the teaching of the Bible, there has been this commitment to social justice, together with the readiness to pay the cost of such involvement — a cost which has invariably included (if not actually been focussed in) the hostility of evangelical Christians who want to keep God out of politics etc. John Wesley, in composing the 'General Rules' for those who were members of his societies and classes, included a prohibition against 'the buying and selling of the bodies and souls of men, women and children, with an intention to enslave them.' He taught that the slave traffic was the greatest of all evils, because it was 'the spring that puts all the rest into motion.' A few days before his death, he wrote to encourage Wilberforce, saying: 'Go on, in the name of God, and in the power of his might; till even American slavery (the vilest that ever saw the sun) shall vanish away before it.'[5]

This link between Wesley and Wilberforce stresses the value of the small group for pressing on and through with a prophetic ministry. If each home church in a given area was prepared to listen to what the Holy Spirit wanted it to do in terms of involvement in the community and, if necessary, challenging the status quo, we would see all over the place a breakthrough for the kingdom of God. We have already noted the presence in any such gathering of Christians of an embryonic prophetic ministry, embodied in one or two who are specially sensitive to the voice of God and declare it without fear or favour. Such members will be very important when a home church is trying to discern what the Spirit is saying about its involvement in the local community.

So often, the prophetic voice is forced out of the church to become a lone voice in the wilderness, over against the church, not committed to it. At times prophets slip out of the Christian community of their own accord, because they find it very painful and difficult for their words to be tested, evaluated and sieved.[6] It is, for many such, a matter of the church accepting all or nothing: if some words are received and others rejected or reserved for later, they withdraw. 'What we need today are prophets who are not afraid to speak out in the name of God, while they remain fiercely loyal to the church as the people of God.'[7]

The awakening and pursuit of a prophetic consciousness in the church is one of the lynchpins of the life experienced by the grassroot communities in Latin America. It would be grossly unjust to their essential character not to stress this feature. A recent English visitor to Brazil starts his report on the communities with an apology:

'Language is always a problem. In this report I frequently use the Brazilian word *conscientizacao*, which is untranslatable into English. It is a key concept in understanding the Brazilian church. The word refers to a process of awakening, of becoming conscious of the nature of society, of learning to perceive social, political and economic contradictions and what one can do about them. But the term does not just refer to consciousness raising. Intrinsic to the process is the idea of taking creative action, of becoming a person who helps to make history, rather than remain a passive object of the decisions of others. It is consciousness-raising with action. . . . Basic to the process is that ideas, action and reflection are inseparable, and that discovery comes through dialogue rather than 'teacher' and 'taught'.[8]

Enough examples of life in the grassroots communities have, hopefully, been already given for this aspect to be readily understood and appreciated. There is, perhaps, no clearer example of the impact of this prophetic consciousness-with-action than these intercessions made at the grassroots community in Contagem, an industrial district of Belo Horizonte in Brazil. While the meeting was proceeding in one part of the building, another part was taken over by security forces:

## Let us pray

'– That we may have the right to freedom of assembly and association, let us pray to the Lord;
  – that there be free and independent unions, let us pray to the Lord;
  – that we may be able to negotiate directly with employers and obtain a just wage, let us pray to the Lord;
  – for a basic living wage, let us pray to the Lord;
  – for an eight-hour day, which our friends asked for as long ago as May 1886, let us pray to the Lord;
  – for most urgent improvements in our rich society, such as sewers, drinking water, street lighting and a proper refuse service, let us pray to the Lord;
  – for a school for our children, let us pray to the Lord;
  – for decent living conditions for slum-dwellers, the sick, and the aged, let us pray to the Lord;
  – for the proper functioning of the police force and the legal system which should protect us and not cause us distress, let us pray to the Lord;
  – that we be able to express our claims, even by strikes, if need be, let us pray to the Lord;
  – that our people, terrified by all kinds of threats, may still

have the possibility and the courage to practise justice and to show kindness to others, let us pray to the Lord.'[9]

Prayer is one of the foundation stones on which the grassroots communities are built. Because prophetic action can so easily become divorced from prayer; because what prayer there is in activist circles can so easily be horizontally directed to rouse the consciences and actions of those present, rather than directed to the Lord to lay the situation before him, and listen to what he has to say and what he wants to be done — for these reasons we need to establish prayer at the heart of the life of our home churches. If the members are truly a cross-section of the church as a whole, in the sense that there will be those at either end and in the middle of the pietistic-prophetic spectrum, there ought to be sufficient stimulus to prevent it becoming unbalanced.

Indeed, it is very important that the prayer-life of a home church ranges far and wide across the world and the church. The Lord's Prayer is a healthy corrective to narrow prayer-concern. It is very valuable to read the local and national newspapers with biblically-informed thinking and in an attitude of prayer, turning together at times to direct intercession. When it comes to specific involvement in some community-need, every initiative must be surrounded in believing prayer: 'Our intercession must be extensive enough to sweep regularly across the whole scene. . . . Like the revolving scanner on a radar scope, discovering the presence of obstacles to the progress of the kingdom of God. Then we must face these mountains, as Jesus told us to, and command them in prayer to move into the sea.'[10] Thus prayer and action are interwoven as a continuous pattern of Christian involvement.

The other perspective on prayer together in a home church has been well summed up thus: 'The establishment of the kingdom of God is an elusive task; we cannot even see what it involves in our vicinity without specific prayer, and we will certainly have little urgency to carry it out unless we are praying.'[11] Because our struggle is not with flesh and blood, but with the spiritual hosts of wickedness, which shelter behind and manipulate people (especially those in authority), all contact and confrontation must be prepared beforehand by the prayer of God's people.

It is instructive to note that Wilberforce and his friends in Clapham regularly spent three hours a day in prayer, and Christians all over England united in prayer on the eve of critical debates in Parliament concerning the abolition of slavery.[12]

Frank Laubach, an American missionary earlier this century, tells of a time spent alone with God on a hilltop in the Philippines. He felt himself to be frustrated in his missionary work and filled with a sense of futility. God met him in a special way that day, leading him to make a commitment to a life of prayer: 'And I added another resolve — to be as wide open towards people and their needs as I am toward God. Windows open outward as well as upward.'[13]

The Vitoria document speaks of the church as leaven or yeast, but 'the leaven of God's new world'. It is easy to slip into a backs-to-the-wall attitude towards this prophetic ministry.

This defensive mentality misses the excitement, the expectancy of being harbingers of God's new world, of actually giving people a little taste of the fullness of God's kingdom. 'Paul views the church as a prism through which the light of the gospel is variously retracted, and those surfaces glitter with all the hidden fire that one day will radiate over the surface of the whole universe. The church, therefore, should not only be a living embodiment of things that happened in the past, but should also luminously reflect the shape of things to come. . . . Nowhere should this be more evident . . . than in the community's meal, particularly when experienced as a real meal with our close Christian family. For this remembers not only the darkness of Christ's death, but anticipates the delights of the Messiah's table. Here amidst sadness and laughter, reflection and conversation, deference and kindness, word and action, eating and sharing, we express the sacrificial love of Christ in our active concern for one another and experience the fellowship of the saints that will one day fill our lives.'[14]

So, the prophetic consciousness-with-action of home churches needs, for its own integrity and sanity, to be rooted firmly in the celebration and prayer of its people. We cannot afford to let the lines of communication between worship and the world become too long. Then, the yeast is outside the dough and has little chance of getting inside — and the dough will never know what exciting and surprising stuff yeast is.

# CHAPTER 12

# A particularly pretty spot

*'There was once a man who lived in a particularly pretty spot in the open country. . . . Lots of people wanted to buy his house, but he would not sell. . . . As time went on, a city was built around his house, but he still kept on insisting he wouldn't move. Buildings were put up, walls and fences, and after a few years there were no trees to be seen, only cement and asphalt. But he remained determined: 'I'm not leaving here because I have a beautiful view. . . .' This is what happens to the church which refuses to budge. . . . The world changes around it, but the church does not move, it simply grows old.'*

We are probably all familiar with the way small groups become so introverted that they are resistant to change of any kind, in almost a more proprietary way than a local congregation. At times, they have justification for such resistance: redirection, new additions, constant re-evaluation and many less disturbing changes are pushed at them from on high, with the result that it is impossible to establish any true community in the Holy Spirit. Even in such a constantly-expanding situation as the home cell units of the Full Gospel Central Church in Seoul, there has been a marked reluctance on many occasions to sub-divide:

'In the beginning of our cell group ministry many people were reluctant to divide. Division had to be forced. That still happens occasionally, but most members . . . realize that the life of the group and of the church depends on constant cell division. Occasionally we have to send one of the pastors to persuade a cell group to divide, but generally the division takes place spontaneously when the group exceeds fifteen families.'[1]

## The Pain of Change

If a home church has genuinely been pushing back the frontiers of what it means to be the church in that area, its members must have found a depth of fellowship and commitment which inevitably makes it very painful to leave one another's close mutual support. Yonggi Cho continues:

'Yes, there are often fears when friends have to separate to attend different meetings, but it is not a life-or-death situation. All of the cell groups are limited to specific geographical areas. If friends are no longer able to see one another in the cell meetings, they still get together at other times of the week, as all friends do, naturally. In addition, there are frequent district activities, where a number of cell groups get together for a picnic, a big prayer meeting or some other event.'[2]

Because, as human beings, we invariably opt for the security of what is familiar, most groups will need more than a little pressure from pastors and others to see multiplication through division as a good thing. It is at this stage — and at many other crossroads in the life of such groups — that the reality of being the church in the home provides an authoritative and creative springboard for growth. If it genuinely is the church, then it is biblically mandated to be both missionary and reproductive in its essential character. Groups which are purely groups can determine their own lifestyle, priorities and lifespan; churches are under the authority of Jesus Christ. This provides a constant stimulus to growth, as well as latent motivation to go out to make disciples. If a (home) church is reproducing its life by making disciples, it will have to sub-divide when numbers preclude its being the church in any realistic way.

## Starting another Church ...

This need not be a cause of gloom and grind: if the home church has been discovering the gifts and potential ministries within its membership, one of the things to emerge will be those who want to 'build with bricks', the kind who are never quite satisfied with the current condition of the home church, who genuinely have it within them to start again somewhere else — along with others. We have earlier called this the modern, deprofessionalised, apostolic ministry. These church-planters are well based in the Scriptures, have a heart for evangelism, know what it is to follow the Spirit, and can look after a small group of believers. Any home church is potentially able to send out such people, at least in pairs, to start another church.

## ... In Costa Rica

An evangelical congregation in a suburb of San Jose, Costa Rica, is a good example of such a ministry. During the last two years or so, it has been responsible for bringing as many as 2,000 people to know the Lord, not least because it is strategically located in the city and therefore can attract newcomers. The main reason for its converting power is, however, the consistent witnessing to Jesus by virtually every member of its congregation, which numbers about 400. In the highly mobile society of Costa Rica, with thousands of people moving between country and city in both directions, a large percentage of these new believers return to the rural areas 12 or 18 months later. The church has a programme of discipleship which takes this social mobility into account. Every convert is placed with a few others in a discipleship course which lasts about nine months. During this time they are taught thoroughly in the path of Christian discipleship. Foundations are laid which are intended to enable each Christian to stand on his own feet, to make his own decisions in the Lord, to take responsibility for his own family and daily life. At the end of this time, many will leave the city. Alberto Barrientos, one of the pastoral team in the church, told me that many new churches have started in rural areas, where there has been no gospel testimony, as a result of these disciples being sent off with such a commission to reproduce.

## ... in Korea

In the suburbs and environs of Seoul, the same story can be told time and time again. 'Our people are so enthusiastic about home cell evangelism that, even when they move away from Seoul, they don't want to leave our church and our cell system. Four years ago, one couple moved to Inchon, which is about 20 miles outside of Seoul. The wife was one of our cell leaders. When we talked, I said, 'Well, I think you should join up with a good church in Inchon.' 'Oh no pastor Cho, that isn't what we want to do at all,' the woman replied. 'I think we will open our house for a cell meeting. Then on Sunday we will all get together and come to Seoul for church.' She has already begun to dream of the successful home cell group she would have at Inchon. . . . Within a very short time they had a thriving home cell group, and on Sunday morning they and their group would all come to church in a chartered bus! Today, that cell group has grown to 130 cells with 2,000 members in Inchon. . . . Today Inchon is a fully-fledged district of our church, with a licensed minister shepherding it.'[3]

### in Britain . . .?

In Britain, in particular, such a concept — let alone such an event — seems unthinkable, not least because of traditional parish boundaries and hypersensitivity to any accusations of fishing in another person's waters or further subdividing the churches into yet another grouping. In what is essentially a pagan country, to be bound by such attitudes and traditions looks perilously like the old man who refused to move when the city was built all around him. When there are such huge tracts of the country where there is no viable manifestation of the living church, it is fundamentally important to plant microcosms of the church in homes everywhere. These will consist of Christians of many different denominational backgrounds, and (hopefully) of none — people who are converted out of nowhere, joining with members of this or that denomination to *be* the church.

It is long past the time when we can be hidebound by inherited denominationalism, particularly in areas of spiritual deadness. It is naturally a different matter when new and independent churches spring up in areas where there is already spiritual life, especially when they are comprised

mainly of disillusioned members of reasonably lively congregations. The escapism and exclusivism of the pure-church
mentality ('we are going to start a church which is really
Spirit-filled, biblical and Christ-centred') is a long way removed from the apostolically-motivated desire to plant a
church where there isn't one worth the name. The evidence of
church history shows all too clearly the folly and the tragedy
of hiving off from existing churches, except when there is
absolutely no alternative.

## A Roman Catholic perspective

The originating dynamics of Central American grassroots
communities are instructive at this point. Dr. Pablo Richard,
who is theological consultant to an interdisciplinary team at
the Departmento Ecumenico de Investigacion in Costa Rica,
spends 10-15 days a month visiting grassroots communities in
Mexico, Panama, Colombia, Honduras, Nicaragua and Costa
Rica (Guatemala and El Salvador are on his circuit, but
internal violence makes them too dangerous to visit). He
explained[4] that the communities originate in one of two ways
— the first is the result of individual Christians looking for a
more personal, participatory and incarnational form of church
life; they come together in homes, or any other suitable
meeting-place, probably under the initiative or certainly with
the encouragement of the local parish priest; the parish
continues to exist, but its life is defined as a network of
communities. Most of this book has been based on this model.

The second way in which grassroots communities come into
being is when Christians who have been dispersed (for several
different reasons) come together as groups in their new area.
Very often in Central America this is due to migration from
the country to the city. In some such areas a new 'barrio' (or
suburb) of 200,000 can emerge in as little as two years. In this
situation there is no such thing as a parish, and so Christians
will spontaneously congregate. Sometimes this will focus
initially on specifically religious activities — to celebrate a
festival, for example. Such a potential grassroots community
could find its initial incentive in some neighbourhood need,
such as a day-care centre for children or a youth club. Still

other grassroots communities begin with Christians involved in political action who feel the need to come together for Bible-study, prayer and mutual support, in order to root their politics in the gospel. In essence, this is little different from the group which met in William Wilberforce's home in the parish of Clapham. Such groups are all spontaneous happenings: Christians *want* to pray together, to study the Bible and to maintain their Christian identity in the local community.

Whether the grassroots communities or home churches originate from the centre outwards, or become established as spontaneous gatherings of Christians in a totally new (to them) environment, the element of readiness for change is paramount. It is not always perceived — and if it is perceived, it is not always readily accepted and welcomed — that change is of the essence of being Christian, being the church. We stop changing when we stop looking to Jesus. Because he is unchanging and unchangeable in his grace, glory and truth, we who are sinful, shameful and false cannot remain for long in his presence without being changed. If this is true of Christians as individuals, it is certainly true of churches. And yet we somehow let ourselves accept that local church life is either not worth changing or does not need changing. We would be appalled if as individuals we found ourselves adopting a similar approach to personal growth into Christ: why do we tolerate resistance to change in the church, either locally or in the home? We need to press out the frontiers of what it means to be the church, never allowing ourselves the fatal luxury of settling down into a rut.

### Ready to move on?

It ought, therefore, to be a primary goal of a home church to plant another home church — either within the same area as part of the network which together comprise the parish, or in a completely different area. In the Portezuelo area of Chile, members of grassroots communities have (in answer to requests from the bishop) twice undertaken responsibilities in other rural areas in order to establish the church in those places.[5] That requires faithful discipleship of the highest order. Such readiness to be changed and even to move on to another place altogether will only happen if such an attitude is already built into the life of the home churches. Dom Helder Camara, formerly archbishop of Recife (Brazil), actually called the communities in his diocese 'Abrahamic minorities', on the analogy of Abraham responding to God's call to move out of the settled life and familiar securities of Ur of the Chaldees, and to go wherever the Lord led him. He certainly did not know where he was going.

## A Worldwide Commitment

One of the very ordinary, but important, ways of keeping a home church looking outwards and prepared to use change creatively is by developing a world-vision for God's work. From time to time it is good for a home church together to plan and to execute a weekend of faith-sharing, renewal or evangelism in another area. The experience will deepen fellowship, refresh faith and stimulate zeal for reproduction. Each home church also needs to be thoroughly committed in support of a missionary working in another part of the world. Such a small body of Christians is uniquely able to take a personal interest in someone who will — already or ultimately — be very well known to them. Letters, tapes, gifts, books, parish newsletters and other magazines all prime the pump of true involvement.[6] When the missionary is home on leave, the home church will be able to welcome him/her/them into their life together — even perhaps to provide accommodation. Imaginative ways can be found, not just of enjoying real partnership in the gospel, but of developing an informed knowledge of the whole situation in another part of the world. It is not impossible, in today's global village, for one or two members of the home church to visit the missionary *in situ*. It might well happen that such a link, prayerfully and joyfully pursued, will actually lead to the home church sending out one of its members as a missionary. Most calls to this kind of ministry coalesce around varied exposure to the situation in another part of the world. In any case, there is a great need for Christians to make themselves informed about what God is doing in other parts of the world, regardless of the possibilty of going there or not. This is particularly true in England, where the attitude still persists that news from other countries is interesting but not particularly helpful for our situation. Nothing is further from the truth.

The need for adaptability, fluidity and improvisation in a home church comes very painfully to most Christians from northern Europe, who have been educated and moulded in an environment which sees planning for the future and achieving goals as of fundamental importance. If we do not use time purposefully, if at the end of the day we cannot point to this or that which we have achieved, we feel that we have wasted time. The Brazilian writer, Gilberto Freyre, points to the Marxist and capitalist common 'obsession' with work. Both systems, he asserts, value human beings on the basis of their material productivity. Atheistic Marxism and Calvinistic Protestantism, he claims, share in 'activism related almost exclusively to time valued in economic terms ('time is money').[7] Latin Americans, I was assured while walking the streets of San José during a time of *fiesta*, see each day as an opportunity to live life to its fullest, and they see personal relationships as absolutely central to a full life. Perhaps this Latin *penchant* can help us to appreciate why there is such a hunger in the West for the kind of fellowship which a home church can uniquely provide. In such an atmosphere the freedom to move at the Spirit's bidding can be truly developed, both in the ongoing life of a home church, and in the bigger challenges to Christian obedience and risk-taking faith. 'Future details are unknown to us; therefore, we are free to improvise as the future overtakes us.'[8]

## Taking risks

Taking risks seems to be at the heart of what it is to be Christian. God himself took risk after risk from the moment he created man in his own image, with the inbuilt freedom to say No to his Creator. God took a risk with Abraham, with Moses, with David: none of them was exactly a paragon of either virtue or reliability. He took the supreme risk in Jesus. However inexorably his purposes were being pursued, to become a man, take frail flesh and die, was to risk everything: 'Jesus risked all and, in fact, when he was crucified, he lost his whole community, all he had achieved in his apostolic life; he did not salvage anything.'[9] If we are ready to risk losing our community, our focus of fellowship and witness, our home church, we will truly find it. We dare not hang on to it.

We dare not hang on to it, or any other part of our lives, because we do not know what might happen to take it away from us. We dare not hang on to individual members of our home church, especially those whose ministry we most appreciate, because they may be removed. This is happening virtually every day in parts of Latin America. In Guatemala, leaders of grassroots communities are being eliminated by government forces, simply because they stand up for the basic needs and rights of the poor — in one case privately related to me with moving simplicity, because he dared to ask and to go on asking for safe drinking water for his people. Christians die in Guatemala, not because they are subversive, but because in the name of Jesus they are claiming basic human rights. The motivation for such a stand is deeply evangelical, i.e. rooted in the gospel; but when motivation turns to action, it is deemed 'political' and subversive. Many grassroots communities in Guatemala, both Catholic and Protestant (and mixed), are painfully learning not to hold on to their leaders or to any of their present resources, but to improvise as the future overtakes them.

The same fluidity and adaptability has characterised the home churches behind the Iron Curtain and in mainland China for many years. In both areas an official church is allowed, if it does not evangelise and keeps within the limits imposed by the State. In Russia, all church members have to be officially registered. Then worship can continue without fear, but under fairly stringent restrictions which exclude, for example, any meeting except the formal worship sessions. In addition, nobody under 18 is allowed to take part actively in the church, and the pastor must have an official licence, the terms of which he must strictly observe. In such a constricted situation, we discover that a city in the Ukraine has a Pentecostal church with over 1,000 'unregistered' members, who meet in 20 or more groups, with up to 50 in each. Group meetings normally move from house to house, to prevent discovery. Each group has a leader and the leaders keep in touch with one another on a regular basis.

We tend to treat such examples as irrelevant because they are remote. If nothing else, however, they underline the power of God to keep his church on the move, to enable his people to alter course, to make adjustments, to improvise. We do not know in the West whether we will face such a situation. We can at least ask ourselves if we are being the church of Jesus Christ in that part of the world where he has placed us. Are we ready and willing to move with the Lord? 'The church which refuses to budge . . . simply grows old.'

# CHAPTER 13

# A bicycle with lots of accessories

*'A bicycle with lots of accessories and trappings ends up by going very slowly. To move fast one has to be light, and so it is with the church — not just a church of the poor, but a church which is poor itself: one without extravagance or pomposity, without trappings and cosmetics.'*

In the majority of cases, the home churches or grassroots communities which have genuinely experienced growth and exerted influence on the world around have been concentrated amongst the poor and the underprivileged. This was true of the 'little flock'[1] around Jesus in which he sought to model the church; it was true of the apostolic church — however influential a few wealthy and well-connected Christians at Corinth might have been;[2] it was true of those integrated into Wesley's classes; it is abundantly true of the grassroots communities in Latin America today. Korea is a Third World country, only one generation on from a war which decimated and impoverished the country.

## The reluctant affluent

It is generally true that the incentive, the imperative, needed to express the life of the church in this way comes very slowly and reluctantly to those who, compared with 75% of the world's population, live in plenty. Paul was able to maintain that he had learned the secret of living with both plenty and poverty, abundance and want.[3] Most of us in the West will admit that we have not been initiated into that liberating secret, whereas many poor Christians do seem to have learned their side of the secret. Both educationally and sociologically we are conditioned to make our own way in the world, to express our individuality in personal assertion, to stand on our own feet as independent, self-resourceful persons. There is obviously much that is Christian in this upbringing, but it usually excludes the mutual interdependence which lies at the heart of the gospel as much as independence.

This privacy and individualism is expressed in a number of ways. First, especially amongst middle-class men, there is a great unwillingness to open up as real people, to be seen to be weak and vulnerable. This fear leads in turn to a veneer of competence, even of coldness. So, in order to reach the real person, you have to break through as well a superimposed crust of reserve and distancing. Such an exterior needs to be reinforced with material possessions and property. This kind of Englishman's home then becomes his castle, into which he withdraws in order to relax and escape from the realities of the world. Added to this double withdrawal, emotional and physical, is a cerebral approach to life's problems and intricacies. We stand outside the situation, glean information from all quarters, evaluate the evidence, and come to a sound, balanced judgement. All these attitudes are the privilege of those with access to educational, social and material resources which provide several options for selection. We then transmit the same attitudes to our involvement in the church: we have a range of options and we exercise our 'right to choose' what kind of Christian fellowship and witness we favour.

An important point to note, by contrast, is that the poor have no such options. They are where they are; they cannot hide from one another because they live cheek by jowl; they have little or nothing to protect or hoard; their lifestyle is predetermined, and they cannot choose either their home, or their job, or their neighbours, or (and this is surely most significant) their church. With such a circumscribed world, there are only two options — in or out: i.e. into the pain and the deprivation with everyone else, or out of it on your own in whatever way you care to attempt. If as Christians you choose to opt into the shared struggle for existence, let alone improvement, you find a strong solidarity and sense of mutual responsibility. You find the church — or at least, thousands of Christians in Latin America are finding the church arising from the grassroots in little communities of committed disciples of Jesus. The combination of a living Saviour and a loving fellowship of believers is, understandably, irresistible and indispensable.

## Four steps forward

If we are not thus situated and if we are not thereby similarly motivated, how do we press ahead with a form of Christian fellowship that at least attempts to move in that direction? In this chapter we want to suggest four steps which can begin, under God, to produce a true *koinonia* of the Holy Spirit — starting with shared experiences of need, weakness, inadequacy and poverty of any kind; going to be with and share with those who are literally poor or on the margins of society; giving away regularly and strategically what is shown to be surplus to our real needs: and receiving ministry from the poor by inviting them to share the true riches with us. If a home church in suburban Britain or America followed these four steps, the Lord would break through the shackles of materialism.

The biggest single danger in all such discussion is that we reinforce our induced guilt over possessing so much when millions starve, freeze and despair. There is no favouritism in the love of God: he loves rich and poor with the same eternal intensity, and Jesus has died to set both free from tyranny of all kinds. The tyranny of guilt he has broken: as the affluent Christian minority experiences freedom from materialism and from the guilt which a sensitised conscience inevitably arouses, and as the deprived majority of Christians are given the opportunity both to share in material blessings and to distribute spiritual blessings, so the Lord's vision for his church will gradually become a reality.

## Share weaknesses

A home church starts, then, with members openly admitting their need of God and of one another. When you have been taught, even programmed, to appear and to be in control, that is a very difficult and threatening place to begin in Christian fellowship. In church after church it has been demonstrated that the breakthrough into true fellowship, and into a new dimension of spiritual reality, comes when those (or the individual) in leadership are released to reveal weaknesses in public. Paul's autobiography in 2 Corinthians enunciates the principles of this in detail, and ought to be compulsory study for home churches. We have grown so accustomed to Christian leadership based on secular models and insights, that we make it incredibly difficult for those over us in the Lord to be human. They, in their turn, make it very difficult for their flock to be real and honest with them and with one another. There is a conspiracy of assumed competence.

It will, therefore, be in the hands of those asked to get a home church off the ground to set the tone from the outset. If, as has been suggested, the opportunity is taken early on to spend time unhurriedly in a weekend away, that provides an excellent atmosphere for real openness. It may be that, to the four Quaker questions mentioned in Chapter 6,[4] we ought to add a fifth: 'Will you share with us one particular need in your own life, so that we can share it with you?' There will be no lack of pains, problems, temptations, weaknesses and anxieties. Then comes the opportunity to share them together with the Lord — 'have no anxiety about anything, but in everything by prayer and supplication with thanksgiving let your requests be known to God': i.e. openness to one another made possible by openness to God and also deepened by openness to God.

Richard Lovelace has written: 'Prayer functions as a safety-valve without which informed Christians would constantly be anxious, aware as they are of the spiritual warfare surrounding them. We might say that we have interceded enough when we have held before God the major responsibilities which confront us and any wider burdens which the Holy Spirit may suggest from day to day, and have exercised faith that he is at work in these. This is not all a difficult labour; there may be times when it can be the work of minutes. Too little prayer is an expression of unbelief in God's love and care; so is too much.'[5]

## Experience poverty

The second step is exposure to the needs of those on the

margins of society. 'As long as we cloister ourselves from the conflicts and tensions of the world, our need of God may remain hidden from us.'[6] We imagine that this need for God is limited to those areas in our lives where we are conscious of not having or being what is necessary for our own contentment. Actually our need for God is far more fundamental and far-reaching than that: we need him in order to break out of an exclusively self-orientated existence, to move from the goal of self-fulfilment to that of declaring his glory and serving his kingdom.

One of the frequently-noted dynamics of the movement into grassroots communities in Latin America is the reorientation of the have's to the have-not's. Indeed, in many places the church as a whole has decisively altered its direction. Until relatively recently the Catholic church in Latin America was automatically a friend of those in power. Now, together with many Protestant churches, it has made a preferential choice for the poor — not excluding the rich, but recognizing in the grassroots communities the work of the Spirit in an irruption of the poor, not just *into* the church, but to *be* the church. Whereas previously the church gauged the effectiveness of its presence by its access to and influence in the various corridors of power, now increasingly it assesses its faithfulness to the gospel in terms of its identification in Christ with the poor. That represents an immense transformation, one which sternly challenges any church which is accustomed to influence and status in the nation — like, for example, the Church of England.

What this revolution in the Catholic church in Latin America has meant in down-to-earth terms is that 'middle-class people come to the grassroots communities and put themselves at the service of the poor in poor areas. . . . We are struggling to open a way amongst middle-class Christians. The danger of this class is to close in on itself: so that our task is to help them open up to others, to enter into communion with more threatened groups.'[7] For the Catholic church this has implied, almost as first priority, a redirection of its full-time personnel towards the poor areas of many dioceses: 'we are not speaking of a presence for charity. . . . A new way of being with the people is being sought. . . . In general, grassroots communities arise from the action of teams of pastoral workers*, whether priests, members of religious orders, or laymen. They act as catalysts for the communal spiritual energies already existing among the people. . . . There is this conversion of pastoral workers to the popular classes — conversion which signifies a faith and confidence in the richness, the value, the capacity of people. . . ; conversion which turns to the people, to live with them and to help them organise themselves as communities of faith.'[8]

What the Catholic church has done — and is doing — in redeploying its full-time personnel, home churches rooted and grounded in Christ are well able to do, in sensitive obedience to the Spirit. The history in England of such Christian exposure to and identification with the poor is the story, in the main, of individual evangelical Christians thus responding to the call of God. The list of such 19th century disciples is almost endless: Lord Shaftesbury's work on behalf of the mentally ill and the homeless poor was as important as his strenuous efforts to stop the abuse of child labour in factories and mines. George Muller, Thomas Barnardo and Charles Spurgeon all took strong initiatives to provide proper care for orphans. Both the Y.M.C.A. and the Y.W.C.A. were started by evangelical Christians to minister to young people moving into the big cities. Pioneering work amongst prostitutes and prisoners was undertaken by such Christians. Important work amongst the deaf and the blind was started by evangelicals (for example, the introduction of Braille).[9] The work of William Booth and the Salvation Army is almost legendary.

## True visiting

What individual Christians initiated in the 19th century home churches are in a position to do today. As James affirms, 'Religion that God our Father accepts as pure and faultless is

* The English phrase 'pastoral worker' is a translation of the Spanish 'agente de pastoral'. This basically means someone who facilitates the mission of the church in any or all of its aspects, not simply pastoral ministry as such.

this: to look after (or visit) orphans and widows in their distress and to keep oneself from being polluted by the world.'[10] Home churches in Cape Town have taken it upon themselves to engage in that kind of ministry on the Cape Flats, going to visit the marginalised of *apartheid* society and supporting individuals sent by the local church as resource medical and social workers.

A more careful study of the word 'visit' is necessary at this point. The Greek word, *episkeptomai*, is used in the Septuagint to combine the various senses of 'visit, look upon, investigate, inspect, test, be concerned about, care for.' It is used particularly of God visiting his people or an individual in order to make known his will either in judgment or in grace. This visitation takes place when God draws near to his people in its sin and distress, and shows himself to be the Lord of history. This distinctive sense is carried over from the Old Testament into the New, cf. the words of Zechariah at the birth of John the Baptist: 'Blessed by the Lord God of Israel, for he has visited and redeemed his people.'[11]

In using the phrase 'I was sick and in prison and you did not visit me,'[12] Jesus makes it plain that such a commitment is basic to being his disciple: 'It is not a question of isolated acts, but of a fundamental attitude. Man has to realize that he does not exist of or for himself, but of and for the other. This is to be expressed in his actions. But God is present in this existence with and for others. Jesus makes this clear when he says that what is done or not done to the least of his brethren is done or not done to him.'[13]

Biblical visiting, therefore, does not mean anything fleeting or superficial, it involves identification, indeed incarnation. It is deep enough and genuine enough to enable the salvation of God to be experienced by the people in that situation. To such visiting we are called as the church of God.

## Give generously

The third step in front of us as home churches is openhanded and openhearted generosity with our material goods. Zacchaeus entered into the joy of his salvation, not only when he made restitution for what he had fraudulently acquired, but when he simultaneously and in addition gave away half of his goods to the poor.[14] We can help one another to look again (or perhaps for the first time) at our wardrobes, libraries, toy-cupboards, larders in the spirit of the two-fold attitude towards possessions mentioned in Hebrews 13: 'be content with what you have . . . share what you have.'[15] We know, both intellectually and instinctively — as well as from experi-ence — that 'happiness lies more in giving than in receiving.'[16] As we give out of our abundance to meet some of the needs of those in want,[17] we will feel the chains of materialism falling off.

It is good for a home church to be committed to both regular giving (perhaps to the work of its own missionary and/or to some more local Christian work) and to spon-taneous offerings. Its life will thus reflect, but not replace, the giving of the local church of which it is a microcosm.

There are, inevitably, two dangers to watch — each at opposite ends of the lifestyle spectrum. On the one hand, joyful contentment and sharing does not mean, nor should it lead to, drabness, scruffiness and meanness. On the other hand, it is not simply a heart-attitude which God is desiring: he does intend us to adopt a lifestyle that is distinctive in very practical ways, not to fool ourselves that our hearts are in the right place when we are not actually prepared to trim our standard of living at all.

## Receive humbly

The fourth step entails the humility to receive, and to go on receiving, from the Lord through the poor. Without this final step, we are still in grave danger of that paternalism which confirms rather than confronts our bondage. It has been a deliberate intention of this book to compel Christians in the West to face up to what God is doing in the Third World. We have an infinite amount to learn and to receive from the church in Africa, Latin America and Asia.

This reversal of historical roles has also taken the church in those continents by surprise. The archbishop of Vitoria, Dom Luis Fernandez, was 'amazed and delighted' to see the document, quoted at the head of each chapter, published in

English. When Paul Yonggi Cho sensed that the Lord was telling him to build an international church growth training centre in order to help pastors from all over the world imbibe the basic principles of the home cell system, he was most reluctant to believe he was hearing God alright.

'I was shocked. 'How can this be, Lord?' I asked. 'I am from a Third World country. We are what is called the 'mission field' by western Christians. Surely such a training centre ought to be built in the United States or Europe.''[18]

Christians in Third World situations, Christians in urban ghettoes, deprived and marginalised Christians can all teach us what being a Christian is all about, what being the church is all about. In a very real sense they can both evangelise and teach us:

'. . . It is the poor who preach the gospel. They have made us understand in new terms that God reveals himself in history and that he does so through the poor. To them God has revealed his love; they are the ones who receive him, understand him and proclaim him.'[19]

There is no value or rightness in calling every person who is poor an inheritor of the gospel promises. But when the poor who know Christ Jesus the Lord share their perception of the gospel, we recognize that we are indeed imprisoned in a narrow understanding of the gospel, which is often more words than deeds. Jesus himself said: 'How hard it is for those who have riches to enter the kingdom of heaven.'[20] That presumably refers not just to initial entry, but to continuous enjoyment of all the riches of the kingdom — its 'righteousness, peace and joy in the Holy Spirit.'[21]

This two-way traffic between the home church and the poor whom we are to visit and welcome holds the key to true enrichment in the family of God. It requires humility in being ready to receive from those . . . . who (so we have been taught) are . . . . in need of our giving. One of the strange paradoxes of being a Christian, which has stood out clearly in this chapter, is that we must learn both to give and to receive.

These four steps, requiring openness, exposure, generosity and humility all find their inspiration in one particular word in the Greek New Testament — *parresia*. In the Greek city-state this was used to describe the essential mark of democracy, freedom of speech. On a more personal level it referred to plainspeaking between friends, without fear or favour. In the New Testament it is used both of Jesus and of his apostles: it indicates openness towards God and towards our brethren, in prayer, in compassion and in trust. It also describes the freedom to speak and to behave before men, especially opponents, without being shackled by fear either of the consequences or of people's opinions. It denotes freedom and confidence, openness and trust, boldness and courage — received as a gift from God through having been fully accepted through his grace in Christ.[22] This is the goal of home church life. Such a church will be better equipped to move ahead with the Lord, without the trappings and accessories which so easily slow us down.

# CHAPTER 14

# Benedict, Lucy and our Lady of the Rock

*'There are many churches round about, whose centre is St Benedict, St Lucy or our Lady of the Rock. That is all very well, and it has its point . . . but (we want) a church which has Christ as its centre. He lives in our midst, and trusts in every single one of us.'*

There has been a very healthy and life-giving investment in shared leadership in many churches in recent years. Instead of the omni-competent superstar, we see teams of elders carrying responsibility for a congregation. Those who have tasted this from the inside would certainly never return to the old pattern. Hopefully, most congregations involved would also prefer this to what they knew before.

It is, however, by no means obvious that this pattern of leadership has either mobilised the gifts of the body as hoped and desired, or significantly pinpointed the headship of Jesus Christ over his body. In some cases, a monarchy has been replaced by an oligarchy. In other cases, there has been a partial recovery of creative ministry, but it has either stagnated or become confined within admittedly wider circles than before, but still confined.

Where there has been division of the congregation into smaller units of the body, home churches or otherwise, the leadership of these units has often become very heavy and dominating. Alternatively, it has been so *laissez-faire* as to be innocuous.

## What is Biblical leadership?

In other words, we do not yet seem to have discovered a true biblical model of leadership. We agree with the people of

Vitoria, that 'we want a church which has Christ as its centre'; but we still stumble along with styles and methods of leadership which have their origins in a secular understanding of how groups of various sizes operate.

In Cape Town we believed strongly as a team in shared leadership. We implemented it as thoroughly as we could. At that time (1974–79), we stressed the need for one person to be '*primus inter pares*', first among equals. That person had no authority outside the team or over against the team, but the buck stopped with him. However much he shared and delegated, he was finally answerable — to the Lord, to the bishop, to the team, to the congregation. In recent years this concept of leadership, however much blessing and benefit may have derived from it, has become increasingly the subject of closer investigation. Several salient ingredients still hold good in this model, but it does not necessarily (or obviously) allow Christ to be at the centre of a church's life nor to be head of his body. In fact, it is all too possible for these 'elders' to become the head and the centre. They are subtly drawn into such a role, and church members also imperceptibly push them in the same direction.

Of course, voices are not lacking to say that any human organisation (and the church, for all its divine origin and vocation, is one such) needs to have one person who is ultimately responsible. Pragmatic commonsense urges the same wisdom, but still the niggle remains: are we letting Jesus be Lord of his church, of this church here and now?

There is currèntly — and probably has been for some time — quite a debate about the pattern of church structure, and especially government, outlined in the Pastoral Epistles. This debate is not about the usual two-tier/three-tier ministry concepts, but about a fairly structured church order as distinct from a more fluid one.[1] I find myself moving more and more into an understanding of eldership which focuses on complementary ministries, rather than on recognized authority. There seems, in any case, to be less and less credibility in any authority exercised from a position of status, whether ecclesiastically imposed or congregationally entrusted. The only authority which works, and which (as we might expect) has biblical mandate, is that which is won by the sacrificial love of those who lay down their lives in the service of others. Such people are 'recognized' by Christians as leaders, because by their unselfishness they set others free.[2]

## Here comes the helmsman again

At this point let us return to the ministry of the 'helmsman', which we explained in some detail in Chapter 5.[3] This gift of steering the home church or the local church was unpacked in the context of the five-fold ministry of apostles, prophets, evangelists, pastors and teachers. Only such a helmsman, it was suggested, can orchestrate these enabling ministries in the body, so that all its latent gifts are fully mobilised. The helmsman is, on this analogy, the enabler of the enablers of the people of God, leaving Jesus by his Spirit to be the true leader.

The example of the grassroots communities in Latin America is most instructive at this point. One of the most common Spanish words for those who enable these communities is *'animador'*, i.e. one who animates or brings life. Most of the *'animadores'* are not full-time workers; usually they are people from the neighbourhood who have emerged from the life of the Christian community as a whole. They are then entrusted with the care of a grassroots community.

The other key person in the network of communities which together comprise a parish is the *'agente de pastoral'*, the person who enables the missionary and evangelistic work of the parish to move ahead. 'The *agente* is neither the chief nor the saviour of the grassroots community. His task is to keep it alive and active and to accompany it in its quest.'[3a] This *'agente'* is normally a priest or full-time worker. In Portezuelo in Chile, the parish priest thus enables the life and witness of 18–20 grassroots communities in his area, that is his main task. Thus, the *'agente de pastoral* enables the *'animadores'*, and each *'animador* enables the members of his grassroots community.

In both cases we can see the enabling ministry as an example of 'helmsmanship', of releasing others into effective service. One of the essential responsibilities of these helmsmen is reflection, reflection on the details of what is happening, as

well as on the needs and potential of each individual. Helmsmen cannot afford to be activists, because then they lose
control of the vessel. They need to be calmly in position at the
right time, making adjustments, reading the signs, giving
encouragement. They should be approachable and available,
with a proper combination of theory and practice.

## Enabling the helmsman

Because the New Testament was written into a home church
situation, this pattern of life will fit most naturally into that
situation. The key question is: what do we do to help
helmsmen be helmsmen? If this is the proper style of leadership, how do we train the leaders? (Another question, of
course, is: who are the 'we' who do the training? But we will
let that one pass!) Helmsmen do not become helmsmen only
by instinct.

In Central America, those who enable the enablers are
gathered together for intensive training. They will, in certain
places, take part in a residential course lasting about 10
weeks. This is divided into three sections: the first is deliberately not related to their specific situation and responsibility.
They will be immersed in the culture of the city where the
training is being held, so that they are in touch with another
scene altogether. Merging their previous experience with this
new exposure, they will then be given the social, political and
economic tools to analyse the reality of everyday life. They are
taught to reflect, judge, act — the threefold guidelines of
grassroots communities.

The second section of the training is spent on the detailed
experiences of being a grassroots community. The purpose,
distinctive characteristics, pitfalls, potential and internal
dynamics are all explored at depth. The whole self-awareness
of the grassroots communities as being the church, not part of
the church, is developed and explained. This learning experience is obviously enriched immensely by the interaction of
'agentes de pastoral' from all over Central America.

The third section of the course is devoted to Bible teaching
and the development of spirituality. This is intended not only,
or even mainly, to give resources for use within the communi-

ties, but to equip the '*agentes*' to be able ministers of the Word
and of the sacraments. This part of the training aims to
increase the spiritual maturity of each person as an enabler of
the enablers of the body of Christ.

It can readily be seen that this 10-week training amounts to
a refresher-course for clergy and full-time workers. They go
back to seminary to learn how to work with grassroots
communities in their parishes, because none of them was
taught about this pattern of ministry in their initial training.

There is also a thorough programme of training both at
the diocesan and at the parish level. Where a diocese has
adopted the pattern of grassroots communities as its basis for
operations, there will be diocesan plans, which include the
setting of objectives, continuous assessment and careful moni-
toring. It is impossible to exaggerate the importance of such
support, encouragement and leadership from diocesan authorities. Where it happens, a pattern of Christian life can
emerge in which a whole region can be impacted with the
gospel: this is happening in certain parts of Nicaragua, where
members of grassroots communities are closely involved with
the radical changes taking place in society after the Sandinista
revolution, and where they are taking full responsibility for
the life of the church — 'the laity virtually run the church.'[4]
Equally, where the recognized authority does not encourage
the grassroots communities, they become less buoyant and
decrease — as is happening in Managua, the capital city of
Nicaragua, because the ecclesiastical powers-that-be are un-
certain, if not afraid, of the impact the church is having,
through the communities, on the whole national situation.

In a parish where there is a network of communities, such
training of the '*animadores*' is crucial. In Portezuelo, Chile,
these people come together for a workshop on the last
Saturday of each month. 'Their main objective is the creation,
formation and strengthening of the grassroots communities;
the formation and ongoing training of their leaders; and
planning for mission (stressing the local, national, continental
and worldwide relationships of the church). A theme is
studied, generally trying to use life events as a starting-point.
The theme is analysed and projected towards all the facets of
life in the grassroots communities through study in small

groups. The Eucharist is vital, and is the focal point of the encounter: efforts continually have been made to make it a real celebration.'[5] Another fiesta!

## A fellowship of leadership

It would never be possible or right to transpose such a pattern of leadership training from Latin America to our own situation. Their approach underlines, however, several priorities and principles which we would be rash to bypass — especially, the crucial need to develop 'a fellowship of leadership' between those at the heart of different home churches, in which thorough training is given, not simply in the mechanics and skills of steering home churches, but in practical discipleship, personal spirituality and mutual encouragement.

A leading question forces itself to the surface at this point: are we prepared to believe that there are such people in our parishes able to become such enablers of home church life? A glance at those responsible for John Wesley's classes and bands should give us great encouragement; a random sampling of early class leaders shows that they included 'a poor peddler, an impoverished widow, a family servant, a carpenter, a schoolmaster-shepherd, a retired soldier, an upholsterer, a tailor, a tanner, a piecemaker, a handloom-weaver, a cordwainer, a cooper, a grocer-breadbaker, and a brazier.'[6]

## Trusting the people

Such was Wesley's measure of trust in those converted through his preaching and discipling ministry, that 'by the time Methodism reached 100,000 members in 1800, the movement must have had over 10,000 class and band leaders, with perhaps an equal or larger total of other leaders. Thus Wesley put one in ten, perhaps one in five, to work in significant ministry and leadership. And who were these people? Not the educated or wealthy with time on their hands, but labouring men and women, husbands and wives and young folks with little or no training, but with spiritual gifts and eagerness to serve. Community became the incubator and training-camp for Christlike ministry.'[7]

This question of trust seems fundamental. The Vitoria document stresses that Christ, who lives in the midst, 'trusts in every single one of us.' Part of what it means to trust in others is to set them free to be the church, the church in the home. Because the church in the home is primary, but not comprehensive, lacking nothing except numbers, it is very important to provide it with the resources which only the local church or wider church can offer. In every way we must seek to let Jesus Christ be manifestly head of his church.

Perhaps the challenge to us is along these lines: if a stranger walked into a meeting of your home church, your staff, your local church at worship, would he immediately recognize who was in charge? Or would he come to the end of the time still unsure, but conscious of somebody else in charge, someone out of sight but very much in the driving-seat? It can happen.

For example, I once visited the staff meeting of a large local congregation in California. There were 15 or 16 people in the room. We spent about three hours together in mutual fellowship, stimulus, banter, teaching and prayer. I had not met anyone in that room before, and I do not know to this day who was meant to be running the meeting. What lives with me is a sense of the leadership of Jesus by his Spirit throughout the morning: there have actually been very tangible results from what happened in the pattern of home-fellowships in that church.

Likewise, it can happen in a congregation met for worship. In a church of perhaps 200 people in San Jose, Costa Rica, I shared in a morning service, which included singing, preaching, testimony, ministry for healing, intercession, sharing of bread and wine, thankoffering and (inevitably) notices. At least 30 people must have taken part at some time or another. At the end, I was left with a true sense of the Lord having been in the midst, but who was responsible for leading it all I know not.

Let the final story come from Latin America — 'After an entire grassroots community in a small town was arrested and brought before the local police chief on charges of subversion, he demanded to be told who was behind them, guiding and manipulating them. They at first replied, 'Nobody. It is all of us that you see here.' The police, unconvinced, insisted, 'Take me to your leader.' They answered, 'The one who encourages us and guides us is our chief. It is our Lord Jesus Christ.' '[8]

# A harvest of potatoes

*'Someone who plants coffee expects coffee, not a harvest of potatoes. . . . A coffee seed first of all becomes a seedling and then a bush, but it is always coffee. In the same way, the church is always the church, but the manner of its being changes. . . .'*

This book is a plea for change. It contains an ideal, an impossible ideal, some would say. I would like to think that it contains a vision, a vision of what the church can become. All over the world Christians are seeking to be the church — effective, compassionate, courageous, faithful. The question is invariably asked: are home churches really the only valid, viable way forward? Rather than answer the question directly, let me rather quote the answer given to a similar question posed to Jose Marins of Brazil; his reply was:

'We should ask, Where does a baptized person live out his Christian experience? He or she cannot live it by himself or herself alone. The church is essentially a community that continues the mission of Jesus. If therefore the church is a community, where is the community of each baptized person? So far we used to answer: in the parish. And so it has been historically. But the parish, as it is now, is too big and it has long ago stopped being a community experience (at least in Latin America). People consider the parish rather like a sort of spiritual 'service station'. They go there to receive the sacraments, to practise their devotions, to fulfil their obligations; but not to have a deep experience of life-sharing or even backing for their mission in the world.

'So for us the question is how to remake the basic tissue of the church, the groundwork of the church, through grassroots communities. It is not simply a movement which is offered to those who like it. We are dealing here with something essential, as if you were asking me: Can a man live without a heart? A man needs a heart, and a Christian needs a brotherhood. The only problem is that the heart — the community — should be healthy and robust.'[1]

Is the state of our church and its groups healthy? Are we gathering a harvest of potatoes, or a harvest of coffee? Remember the aroma of freshly ground coffee? 'We are the aroma of Christ.'[2]

# The Church the people want

(Document from the Archdiocese of Vitoria, Brazil)

In the Archdiocese of Vitoria the Church is changing. It is a change in kind. Take a coffee seed, for example. First of all it becomes a seedling and then a bush, but it is always coffee. In the same way the Church is always the Church, but the manner of its being so changes. The seed is different from the plant, and the plant is different again from the fruit. Now the Church in the diocese of Vitoria is planting a seed in that soil which is the life of the people. A seed always stays beneath the soil. No one sees it, it is even possible to walk over it. But given time it begins to germinate within the soil, that is, within our lives. And after another while it is going to sprout. What is it that makes it spring into life?

What sort of fruit do we hope for from those seeds that the Church is planting in our communities? Someone who plants coffee expects to harvest coffee, not a harvest of potatoes. So let us see what harvest it is we are all hoping for from those seeds the Christian community is sowing in the soil of our lives, in our cities and in the countryside.

## The Church is the people of God

A Church can't be made up simply of priests. In fact, of course, it is mainly made up of lay-people. An architect may know how to construct a house, but it is a gang of workmen that actually builds it. An architect's plans aren't enough — they are only on paper, and no family can live on a piece of paper: it lives in a house of stone or of brick or of wood or of compacted earth. The house is put together through the work of the bricklayer, the carpenter, the gas-fitter, the electrician and so on. However, a house that is put up without the aid of plans and calculations turns out badly, so the architect is important — but he doesn't built it on his own. That is the way of the Church. The priest is important, but he on his own isn't the Church, not does he create it. The Church is all those who have faith in God and love for their neighbour. Within the Church everyone has his place and carries out his task, just as in the construction of a house. So someone takes charge of the chapel, someone else lends his house for community meetings, someone else again organises the celebrations, one lady visits the sick, another reads and explains the Bible to the community, a girl teaches the catechism to children and so on. The priest is like the architect. He encourages and helps to guide the community, but any job can be done without the constant presence of the architect. The workmen know their own trades. In the Church it should be the same, everyone knowing how to carry out his or her own task. All are responsible together, priests and laity alike. No one is better than anyone else, all have equal importance. Christ is master of the house: each one of us is a brick in its building.

## A people's Church

A Church is made up by people, and that doesn't mean just by the people who have money or position. Jesus was poor, the apostles were poor — many of them were fishermen — and the Church, too, ought to be poor. Humble, simple people ought to hold the first place within it. Just as Jesus gave preference to the poor, so the Church ought to give preference to ordinary people, to factory workers and farm labourers. In the world about us the poor serve the rich: in the Church the rich ought to serve the poor.

## A small Church

It is better to be bothered about quality rather than quantity: a tiny diamond is far more valuable than a lorryload of stones. It is for that reason that we are going to work with groups and small communities rather than with large crowds. There are plenty of people who are Catholic only in name. They are not involved with the Church unless there is a child to be baptized or a girl to be married — and even they get worked up if the priest doesn't do it the way they want. No, we are only concerned with small communities made up of people who know they are the Church. It is with these that we are going to set about the work of spreading the Gospel, of proclaiming in word and deed that Christ came to free us from wretchedness and oppression, whether that be spiritual or material. Work in small groups is far more worthwhile. A spoonful of sugar dissolved in a small cup sweetens the coffee, and that is the way with the Gospel in a small community. But put the same spoonful of sugar into a huge pot of coffee and its taste simply gets lost.

## A community Church

There is a difference between a crowd and a community. A church may be packed with people hearing mass, but it is quite possible they have nothing in common, they are simply a crowd. In a crowd one person is alongside another. In a community people constitute a group in contrast to others, they have something in common. Imagine a family which has fifty members. Some members can hardly be acquainted with the others. In a family of five, however, everybody knows everybody else. That is why we have to create, encourage and give life to basic ecclesial communities. Where Christians from the same street, the same part of town or the same place of work can come together, there we have a basic ecclesial community, a Church community.

## A Christ-centred community

That sounds very complicated, but it means something quite straightforward: a Church which has Christ as its centre. There are many churches round about whose centre is St Benedict, St Lucy or Our Lady of the Rock. That is all very well, and it has its point because Benedict, Lucy and Our Lady were all people who completely lived out what Christ had taught, but you can't swop a car's motor for a whole lot of accessories. A car runs on its engine, and in the Church Jesus Christ is the engine, Jesus Christ dead and risen for us. He lives in our midst, and trusts in every single one of us.

## A Church of the Laity

We have already seen how, just as it is not simply the architect who builds a house, it is not merely the priest who makes the Church. The Church is the laity, the people. Some lay people have gone on to become priests, and then have been appointed bishops, even Pope — Pope John XXIII was a poor peasant from Italy. They haven't taken these jobs on so that they can order people about, but so that they could serve the laity. The Church is made up of everyone who has faith. It is not enough to know that one belongs to a family. One has to feel a commitment towards, and feel a responsibility for, the growth of that family. The laity ought to have an increasing say in the running of the Church, because they are the Church.

## A personalised Church

That is, one in which everybody feels they are really some-body. You can set off on a journey and come to a town where you hang about in the town-centre talking to no one, knowing no one. In that case, it's quite likely you won't enjoy the trip. But if, when you arrive at a town and go along to its centre you talk to people, then you will enjoy it because you have been recognised as a person. That is the way it ought to be in the Church: everyone with a name and a face. Yet there are still people in the Church who feel themselves to be shoppers in the great supermarket of the faith: they go along only to buy baptisms, nuptial masses and funerals. Others who come along to the Church appear only to have ears because they never open their mouths to speak. Yet others seem to have left their bodies at home — they are all soul, as if salvation was to do only with the soul and not with the whole person. Very well then, God wants to liberate the entire human being from his material misery as much as from his spiritual misery.

## A charismatic Church

That, too, sounds pretty complicated, but it means a Church where the Holy Spirit can blow where it wills and brings life, not a Church full of rules and structures and mechanical rituals. You can buy and plant the best sort of seeds, and purchase the very best sprinkling machine. But if the seeds aren't watered every day, and if the sun doesn't shine, then plants are going to die. The Church may be all very fine and well-organised, but if it lacks the water which is the faith of the people and the sun which is the Spirit of God, it grows weak. It will sink down like a wheel which is stuck in the mud and skids round and round in the same place. The Holy Spirit shows every member of the Church what he or she is capable of, and how each one can help the community: the tasks and duties we were talking about a few moments ago. These are charisms, that is, the gifts which God has handed out to individuals for the good of all. That is how the Church is going to make progress.

## A pluralist Church

'Plural' means many: Christians. 'Singular' is only one: a Christian. A pluralist Church is one which doesn't stay turned in on itself, like the owl which hides itself away, but which opens itself to everyone around it, and welcomes the help of all. A Church which values the different pastoral experiences, the various ways chosen by the different communities. A good salad isn't just made of lettuce. It has in it potatoes, green beans, carrots, peppers and mayonnaise. This is how it become a good salad. And that is what should happen in the Church: it ought to be able to make the most of the qualities and work of each person so as to give a chance to all.

## A local Church

Or rather, one with local characteristics. There are thousands of yellow Volkswagens in Brazil, but every owner knows perfectly well which is his because, although the cars all look alike, each has its own peculiar characteristics. Our Church, likewise, ought to have its own special features, its own qualities, its particular way of operating. That is how it is going to contribute best to the Church throughout the world, the universal Church.

## A poor Church

Not just a Church of the poor, but a Church which is poor itself: one without extravagance and pomposity, without trappings and cosmetics. A bicycle with lots of accessories and trappings ends up by going very slowly. To move fast one has to be light, and so it is with the Church. At the same time our Church ought to be humble and unpretentious, making no claim to have sole rights on the truth or on salvation (the crystal balls of the fortune tellers). A poor Church, if it hasn't got chapels, meets in houses, if it hasn't got loud speakers set high up on the church towers will make do with some lad's guitar, a Church which, if it needs help, asks people for it.

## A pilgrim Church

There was once a man who lived in a particularly pretty spot in the open country. Lots of people wanted to buy this house, but he would not sell:

'I'm not moving, because from here I can contemplate the beauty of nature'. He had a point, but as time went on a city was built around his house, and he still kept on insisting he wouldn't move. Buildings were put up, walls and fences, and after a few years there were no trees to be seen, only cement and asphalt. But he remained determined: 'I'm not leaving here because I have a beautiful view'. This is what happens to a Church which refuses to budge, staying always in the same place. The world changes around it, but it does not move. The world renews itself, the Church simply grows old. A pilgrim Church is one which has feet for walking, and is always setting off into the future. So this Church is always revising its style of life, always undergoing a process of renewal, always questioning every step it takes so it never grows old and rusty. The oil which keeps its gears in working order is made up of two things, the gospel and life itself, that is to say, the words of Jesus and the events and situations which reality goes on putting in front of us.

## An ecumenical Church

We Catholics are not the only people who believe in Jesus

Christ. Protestants follow him too — Baptists, Seventh Day Adventists, Presbyterians and so on. They are just as much Christians as Catholics are. So the Church ought to try to live in unity with other Churches. God doesn't want division; he wants unity, for in unity there is strength.

## A missionary Church

The Church is like a bus. No one gets on a bus to walk up and down it but to be carried from one place to another. A bus is a vehicle as well, one that carries us towards the Kingdom of God. The mission of the Church doesn't lie within itself, but outside it. It is to proclaim the presence of the Kingdom of God within the world of men. No one talks for his own benefit but to be heard by others. So the Church lives and preaches the gospel to transform the world, and to transform men.

## A Church made flesh

Every community which goes to make up the Church of a particular place, whether it be of a city, a district or a household, ought to put down roots in that place. A rootless Church is like an up-rooted plant: it will soon wither away. Everything that troubles people ought to concern the Christian community. If from some place the inhabitants are driven out, then the Church ought to share their problem. If somewhere else there is no water or no electricity in a poor district, the Christian community ought to share in that problem too. And so ever onwards. No progress is going to be made merely by praying a lot, if Christians do not take men's problems on their shoulders, just as Jesus did.

## A dynamic Church

Stagnant water breeds insects, it is bad for the health. But running water is clean, anyone can drink it. A Church which is turned in upon itself, closed in within its own structures, is just like stagnant water: it cannot slake the thirst which men have for God. A dynamic Church, on the other hand, one committed to men's problems, is like running water: it slakes the thirst and renews men's strength.

## A living Church

Just as plants live off water and the sun, so the Church lives off faith and life. These two ought to be linked together. People should look upon the happenings of everyday life as faith-events. That is, the things that happen ought to be celebrated in faith: a good harvest, a friend's birthday, the companionship of one's workmates, the rejoicing over the local team's victory, the co-operation involved in helping to build a house for a neighbour, and so on. All these things ought to be as much a part of Christian celebration as the birth of a child is celebrated in baptism, or someone's entry into adolescence is marked by confirmation, or we celebrate in the Eucharist Christ being made the food for life, or, in matrimony, we celebrate the union of love between a young couple, and so on. The sacraments number more than seven. Every event in our lives is a sacrament, if it serves to bring us nearer to God and to men.

## A servant Church

Jesus said he came to serve, not to be served. A Christian community is not here to be served either, but to serve. Someone who does not live to serve does not serve for anything; someone in these parts once said 'To think of a Christian who doesn't want to serve is like thinking of a chauffeur who doesn't know how to keep hold of the steering wheel'. And the Church serves the people by sharing in their search for liberation. Man ought to be free from wretchedness and oppression, from ignorance and disease. Jesus gave sight to the blind, made the lame walk, restored lepers to health and the dead to life. So the Church ought to serve, and to free, those who today need its love most: the poor.

## A Church as leaven

The kingdom of God is a phrase used in the Bible to mean the world which, one day is going to exist. God has promised it. It is a world without wretchedness, without division between rich and poor, without the deaths of young children. It means a world here on earth in which all men will live as brothers, each one trying to serve the others. Now the Church is the leaven of this new world, the yeast put into the dough so that it will rise. A Church remote from the world is like yeast outside the dough. In its own particular city, district or place of work, each Christian community should be the leaven of this new world. It ought to be denouncing every barrier in the way of communion among men. It ought to throw down every obstacle dividing the people one from another. A Christian wants a world without privileges. He wants a world where everyone can have the same rights: we are all equal in the sight of God. It is the Church's task, therefore, to fight for this world. It has to look out for, and draw attention to, all the things that give rise to difficulties in building this new world. That is why Jesus told us to pray each day: 'Thy kingdom come.'

## A prophetic Church

In the Bible a prophet isn't somebody who foretells the future. He is someone who points out to others what the will of God really is. That is the vocation of the Church in each ecclesial community: to show people what really is God's will. It is not the will of the powerful, who only want to give orders and increase their wealth. It is the will of Jesus Christ, who made himself poor among the poor. Just like Jesus, the community ought to denounce the mistakes and injustices committed by society. When a Christian is silent, then God is silent, because he wants to speak through our mouths.

## A liberating Church

A man isn't spirit alone. If he were, he wouldn't need to work in order to eat. Man is flesh and bone, he has conscience, memory and understanding. Therefore the Church isn't out to save merely what is spiritual in man, but it wants 'to save the whole of man, and the whole of mankind' (Paul VI). To save means to liberate: to liberate from both spiritual and material wretchedness. Within society, the Church should be the voice of those who have no voice, trying to make a more brotherly and just world. It is a task which it ought to undertake with courage, because Jesus had no fear of the cross: it was on the cross that life was to be found. The cross, persecution, calumny and slander, these are the glory of a Christian. They show him that he is on the side of the poor, and not on the side of those who want to maintain poverty so that they themselves can become more wealthy. 'Blessed are those who suffer persecution for my name's sake' (Mat. 5).

# 'One Finger does not kill a louse' –

Establishing Basic Christian Communities in Lusaka, Zambia
The Experience of Father A. Edele, 1971–77

The following is an account of my experiences in connection with basic Christian communities since 1971.

In 1968 I had become parish priest of St Charles Lwanga Parish in Chilenje, one of the suburbs of Lusaka. Of the 42,000 people living within the parish boundaries about 10,000 were Catholics. At the time of my appointment I had very little pastoral experience, and none at all in respect of urban parishes. I therefore scrupulously followed the advice of my predecessor: 'The most important duty of a pastor in town is parish visitation.' It took me three years to make the round of the parish and I was proud when I finally had a complete *status animarum*. During my visits I had succeeded in persuading a great number of Christians to resume their Sunday duties and quite a few to straighten out their irregular marriage situations.

Early in 1971 I started my second round of visits, but soon realized that much of my previous effort had proved futile. Nearly 50% of the population had moved in the meantime, so that I was continuously knocking at the wrong doors. The carefully compiled *status animarum* was out of date. Many other Catholic families had moved into the area, and quite a number of those who had resumed their Sunday duties, as a result of my previous visit, had quickly lost their fervour.

Another realization made me question the usefulness of family visitation. In a small street of 20 houses I discovered 14 families who professed to be Catholic. Thirteen of them, however, knew only *one* other Catholic family in their street, namely, that of a member of the Legion of Mary, who visited them regularly. If Christianity meant brotherhood, then Christianity was almost totally absent from the parish despite the fact that 10,000 Catholics lived there. In other words, the witnessing aspect of Christianity was practically nil. I decided to look for ways and means of solving these problems.

## A first attempt at forming Christian communities

There were two lay organizations in the parish that were quite keen to visit lapsed Catholics. Though the members were very zealous, proper organization was lacking and, consequently, one family might be visited during the same week three times by different groups, whereas others received no visit at all. I intended to channel this zeal to a more useful purpose. I therefore divided the parish into units of 50–60 houses, on the assumption that in each unit there could be found 15–20 Catholic families, and assigned one or two members of the lay organizations to each unit. They were to visit every single house and compile a simplified *status animarum* covering every Catholic family in their unit. They went about their work with enthusiasm, and within four weeks I had in hand a complete survey of the Catholic population of the parish. I then asked them to gather the Christians of their units and discuss with them the practical means of witnessing to their Christianity in their surroundings. Unfortunately I neglected to prepare them sufficiently for this task. They were soon at their wit's end and asked for the priest's presence at these meetings. Even though I did everything I could to be present at some of the meetings, I was incapable of attending them at all. Thus the workers got tired, and what has started with enthusiasm ended in discouragement and a sense of failure. However, I did not give up the idea of forming such communities.

## A more humble beginning

In 1973 a Sister was appointed to the parish as a full-time pastoral worker. I proposed forming a real team with her and the parish catechist. Together we worked out a pastoral programme for the parish. Its main orientation was the formation of small Christian communities. But this time we wanted to prepare ourselves thoroughly.
*Preparation:*

We got valuable hints on how to form Christian communities from descriptions of experiments in Europe and South America, even though we fully realized that there was no use in trying to copy them, since most of those experiences involved only a small percentage of the Catholic population, whereas we wanted, as far as possible, every Catholic family to take part. We decided on a small formation programme and selected themes for discussion at initial meetings. The themes were mimeographed in booklet form, in the vernacular, so that they could be kept by the communities for future reference. Finally, we selected three of the previously established units in different areas of the parish to start the experience, hoping that these communities, once established, would radiate their influence into neighbouring units.

A first contact:

It took us about two weeks to visit every Catholic family in each unit. During the visit we explained our intention of bringing Christians in their area into closer contact with one another and invited them to a meeting in the house of one of their fellow Christians. Usually, about three-quarters of the families visited turned up at these meetings.

*The programme of the initial meetings:*

At the first meeting each one introduced himself to the others. We then invited everybody to talk about the problems they were facing in living their Christianity in town. As isolation was one of the problems most commonly mentioned, we were able to explain the basic Christian communities could provide an answer to their needs: and very often a spontaneous request followed for a continuation of these gatherings.

At the next 7 or 8 meetings one member of the parish team would be present to animate the discussions, which were on the following topics:

– the purpose of a Christian community,
– the first Christian communities as described in the Acts of the Apostles;
– the Church as instrument of salvation;
– the Church as the 'tribe of God';
– the natural tribe compared with the 'tribe of God';
– Baptism as birth into the 'tribe of God';

– the Eucharist as a 'meal of communion'.

This series of meetings was followed by the celebration of the Eucharist with the group as a visible expression of its now being a Christian community.

*Establishing community structures*:

During these initial meetings the community had already become aware of some of the tasks and responsibilities Christians have within their community and their own surroundings. We therefore proposed that each and every family should take charge of one of the 'services' needed within the community. They usually started by choosing an 'elder' for their community and then shared out the other tasks, such as caring for the sick and for the poor; visiting and inviting newcomers to join the community; visiting lapsed Catholics; arbitrating in family disputes; initiating catechumens to Christian life; encouraging children to attend the parish catechesis; administering community funds.

*Animating established communities*:

The communities usually met once every fortnight but quite a few opted for weekly meetings. As the parish team continued founding new communities, it became increasingly difficult for us to attend all the meetings. We began, therefore, to have monthly meetings with the 'elders'. The main aim of these meetings was to give the 'elders' a chance of exchanging their experiences and to discuss together the problems they encountered in their respective communities. At the time, we introduced them to simple principles of leadership and gave them practical lessons in Bible-sharing. As a result of these meetings we slowly worked out a pattern for the meetings within the communities.

At least one meeting per month was devoted to *the deepening of their faith*. For this purpose we prepared some booklets with outlines for Bible-sharing. Each booklet contained material for several sessions on one theme such as, for example, 'The risen Christ is the cornerstone of our faith'; 'Christ is really a man like us'; 'To be a Christian means to be Christ-like'; 'A Christian continues Christ's work'; and so on.

A second meeting every month would be devoted to discussing means for *strengthening brotherhood* within the community. Each member would be invited to make known to the community some personal problem or difficulty and the community would try to find ways and means of assisting whoever was in need. Here the Community Fund came in very handy. Encouragement was also given to the practice of celebrating together happy events such as births, the coming of age of a girl, marriages, etc. On such occasions, or if a person were sick over a long period, a Eucharistic celebration might be arranged in the community, and often neighbouring communities were invited to attend.

If, at a Bible-sharing, the community came to a new awareness of the Christian's responsibility in society, we asked that one or two meetings be set aside for the deepening of this awareness, so that people could discover how social evils affected individual lives.

## A first evaluation

In the year or so since the beginning of our pastoral programme, we had gathered enough experience to be confident that we were on the right track, when suddenly I was called to Europe. The Sister had to take over the whole parish administration and had very little time left to visit the existing communities, much less to form new ones. For six months the established communities were left without any special attention. This was the first test the communities had to pass.

What was the situation when I returned six months later? Of the 20 Christian communities we had managed to found in the first year, thirteen were still functioning without any major difficulty, four were still active but required new stimulation, two had virtually collapsed and one had completely disintegrated. Valuable information came to light as we searched for the reasons for the varied degrees of failure or success. In one instance a member of one of the lay organizations, resenting the fact that he had not been chosen as an 'elder', had successfully undermined that community. In another case, tribal clashes had played a major part in weakening the community. The other five communities that had weakened were all situated in an area where the majority of the people belonged to the lower middle class. It thus became evident that the lower income bracket and general education of the people, the better the chance of creating a community spirit, in spite of the fact that among the less educated it was often difficult to find an 'elder' proficient enough at reading to use the material provided for Bible-sharing and other information. These findings were confirmed a few months later, when a completely different experience in community-building came my way.

## A new experience

Shortly after my return from Europe (1 March 1975) I was replaced as parish priest of St Charles Lwanga, and was appointed to take charge of a large shanty-town on the outskirts of Lusaka, called Mandevu. The population, estimated at between 35,000 and 40,000 included 8,000 Catholics. From the very beginning, Mandevu, being an out-station of an urban parish, had received only a minimum of pastoral care. For more than a year before my arrival such care had amounted to no more than an occasional visit by one or another priest who happened to be in Lusaka over the week-end. Church life had somehow survived, due to a Church Committee composed of some active Catholics. Church attendance was rather low and the general state of affairs lamentable. The great majority of marriages were not blessed in church, many youths and even adults had not been admitted to First Communion. I envisaged a minumum of two years of effort at remedying the situation before even thinking about forming Christian communities. As it turned out, things developed quite differently.

The existing Church Committee was transformed into a Parish Council, and it was here that I explained the long-term policy of establishing Christian communities. The members asked me to furnish them with the literature which had been prepared in St Charles Lwanga parish, and only a month or so later they surprised me with the news that they had started to establish Christian communities in different areas of the parish. I did not want to discourage such initiatives, but, remembering my previous experience, I did not envision much chance of successs. Though I could not find time to visit these communities, they continued to meet regularly, and the number of communities increased as other Christians caught on to the idea. Towards the end of 1975 I was fortunate enough to receive a community of three Sisters in the parish. In view of the enthusiasm with which they were welcomed by the Christians, we decided to give priority to the Christian communities and try to renew parish life through them. This, however, was not possible, as we well realized, unless we found ways to strengthen the infrastructures of the parish at the same time.

## The secret of success: training of the laity

Together with the parish council we discerned four areas in which development would have to take place: Christian communities, catechesis, liturgy and family life. Each member of the parish team was given responsibility for one of these aspects. Together we planned a programme of 20 training sessions for each topic, and selected suitable candidates for training. 156 Christians assisted with astonishing faithfulness at these fortnightly sessions from February to November 1976. To describe in detail the contents of these sessions would take too long. Suffice it to say that they were conceived in such a way that the trainees were able to put into practice, without much delay, whatever they learned. By April of that year we were able to organize the week-end catechesis for all the children of Catholic families, set up a Council for marriage preparation and marriage guidance, and introduce para-liturgical services for children, as I was not always able to celebrate the Eucharist with them. Needless to say, the 'elders' of the Christian communities put their newly found knowledge into practice from the very beginning.

As the workload of the parish team diminished, we found time to attend most of the meetings of the Christian communities, all four of us sharing in this task. As a result, we discovered at grassroots level the different needs of the population of the parish area.

We evaluated this experience at the end of the year and worked out another training programme for 1977. One Sister started to train ladies in different household skills so that they in turn could establish Women's Clubs in their respective communities. It was, of course, impossible to train all the ladies of the parish at the same time. Another Sister set up a Bible-study course with one or two participants from each Christian community in order to facilitate the deepening of the faith within the communities through Bible-sharing. The third Sister took charge of organizing the youth, as she had some previous experience in this field. I was left free to deal with the ever increasing administrative work at the parish office, especially since at that time a start was made on building a parish church. We did, however, continue to call together at least once a month the groups we had trained previously.

## Reflections

Having reported somewhat succinctly my experience in community-building in Mandevu parish, I would like to make a few reflections on this experience that might prove helpful.

Let me start with a personal confession: I am more a methodical organizing type than a charismatic, which is not always an advantage in this work of establishing Christian communities. Hence my somewhat painful experience before I realized that the Spirit can blow in directions which may be disconcerting. The following reflections will help to understand what I mean.

a) One cannot *build* Christian communities: they must *grow*. A building is constructed from a preconceived plan, but a tree grows, and no two trees, even of the same species, will grow to the same shape. In the same way Christian communities must be allowed to grow from within their own resources. Endeavours to make them develop according to a predefined plan will stifle or even suffocate them. Just a few examples to demonstrate this.

In St Charles Lwanga Parish we had portioned out the parish into units and foreseen one community for each unit. When members of the Mandevu Parish Council started their Christian communities, they gathered Christians from an area which, in my view, was far too big. But, whereas we had more or less 'forced' Christians to take part in the community, they had gathered those who were willing and eager to participate.

As a result, even today, after seven years of community-building, St Charles Lwanga Parish still has areas where Christian communities are not yet established, whereas the whole area of Mandevu parish was covered within two years. Naturally, most of the communities in Mandevu had to split up as membership increased, but this presented no difficulty. I estimate that today between 70 and 80% of the Catholic population of Mandevu takes part in community meeting. I am not able to assess the rate of participation at St Charles Lwanga Paish.

Another example: We naturally presumed that a Christian community comprised men and women, but usually the participation of men left much to be desired. One of the reasons, we were told, was the difficulty of finding a time for meetings that suited the men. After some hesitation we allowed women and men to meet on their own, provided they would have joint meetings from time to time. Besides increasing the participation of men in the meetings another advantage was gained we had never thought of. In traditional African society men are considered the spokesmen for the family in any gathering, whereas the women are supposed to keep silent. Even though we encouraged women to speak up at Christian community meetings, it carried very little effect. But now, as women met on their own, they dared to speak up and form their own convictions, and they were less shy to voice them at the periodic joint meetings. In some places communities have returned to the practice of meeting together all the time.

A third example: In a particular area of the parish it was nearly impossible to get men to attend meetings despite many efforts on my part. Suddenly, after three years of having a community of women only, the men came to ask for help in getting their own meeting started. Today this community is as flourishing as the others.

Finally: in our efforts to bring as much uniformity as possible, we had asked the 'elders' to select Christians to be responsible for the different 'services' within the community. Though this was done, the people selected proved usually not very active in their respective fields. It was only after each community grew and felt the need for such 'services' — and these needs differed from community to community — that ways of their own to provide for them in an effective manner were developed.

b) 'One finger does not kill a louse'. This African proverb expresses most adequately the experience I passed through in my endeavours to establish Christian communities. The proverb expresses two things: first of all, you need at least two fingers to kill a louse, and secondly, not every finger is equally dexterous for doing the job. Or did you ever try to kill a louse with your little fingers? On the other hand, another proverb has it, that 'you need the little finger to pick your nose'.

What do I mean? We priests have been trained to be 'in charge' of a parish and we interpret this as meaning we have the final word in everything that goes on in the parish. We are willing to hand over responsibilities, provided we can keep control, under the pretext that after all we are held responsible for anything that might go wrong in the parish. If we insist on this often enough, our collaborators will resign themselves to the fact, with the result that we prevent them very often from using their talents and expertise to the full.

I have been lucky to have had a team of collaborators during most of the time I was 'priest in charge', but it took me a long time before I was ready to en-'trust' to them full responsibility for certain aspects of the work in which they were more experienced or more talented. But having learned the lesson — and I am still in the learning process — I venture to say that any effort at establishing Christian communities in a parish will only be successful to the extent that we, priests, are prepared to be part and parcel of the 'first Christian community', which is the parish team.

(Taken from Pro Mundi Vita Bulletin No. 81, April 1980)

APPENDIX C

# Two tidy summaries

Tidy minds like a neat summary of everything. Here are two such examples related to home churches, one from the United States, the other from Tanzania.

*7 marks of 'a biblically-based community in the world today'*

1. It should be genuinely evangelical, committed to the gospel and drawing its principal inspiration from the Bible
2. It should be a small-scale model of the church, thus visibly demonstrating the reality of the Christian community
3. It should be an agent of reconciliation between the churches, being in the proper sense catholic as well as evangelical
4. It should be outreaching, with an evangelistic missionary fervour
5. It will be in conflict with the principal values and spirit of the surrounding culture, thus demonstrating the line between the church and the world
6. It should be an eschatological sign of the coming kingdom of God by its radical witness to the lordship of Christ
7. It should give time to study and instruction as well as prayer and proclamation

(Taken from Donald Bloesch, *Wellsprings of Renewal* (Eerdmans, 1974), pp. 108–112)

*Pastoral Schema for Tanzania (1981)*

1. Formation of small Christian communities — neighbourhood groupings of extended families in rural areas. The distinctive characteristics are a *praying community* (participating in the weekly Bible Service) and a *sharing community*

(the socializing, home visiting, exchange of goods and services, etc.) connected with interpersonal relationships and familyhood ('Ujamaa' in Swahili) values.

2. Communities begin to reach out to others especially the poor and needy in their small communities or in the wider community. The *serving community* provides material goods and proceeds (in cash or crops) from the small Christian community farms for the poor and volunteer help to the needy. It also participates in various social-economic development projects.

3. As its identity develops the community begins to·reflect on its life and the Gospel. The *reflecting community* either starts with Scripture and goes to life or starts with life (local proverbs, African customs and traditions, concrete village experiences, etc) and goes to the Scriptures.

4. The small Christian community develops a missionary thrust. The *evangelizing community* reaches out to other less-developed communities with pastoral animation, home visitations, formation seminars and material assistance.

5. Deeper reflection on its social-economic-political reality creates a *liberating community* involved in social change, action for justice and solidarity with the poor and oppressed. Prophetic witness and action directed toward racism (tribalism), inequality between the sexes, corruption, exploitation, bribery, Black Market economy, superstition and witchcraft.

# Notes

*Introduction*

1. Cf. Charles M. Olsen, *The Base Church* (Forum House Publishers, 1973), pp. 33–40.
2. See his book *Disciple*.
3. Information about the church in China is gathered by a special research centre in Hong Kong.
4. *Pro Mundi Vita Bulletin* No. 81 (April 1980), p. 35.
5. Ibid., pp. 35–36.
6. John and Karen Hurston, *Caught in the Web* (Church Growth International, 1977), p. 19.
7. Bill Cook, *The Expectation of the Poor* (Dissertation submitted for Doctor of Philosophy degree at Fuller Theological Seminary, Pasadena, California, 1982), p. 3.
7a. Joao Libanio, *Putting Theology to Work* (Conference for World Mission, 1980), p. 35.
8. Ibid., p. 183.
9. Jose Marins, one of the leading commentators from within on the grassroots communities in Brazil, interviewed for *East Asian Pastoral Review*, February 1982, pp. 60–61.
10. J. B. Libanio, quoted by Bill Cook, op. cit., p. 212.
11. Jose Marins, quoted by Bill Cook, ibid., p. 226.
12. Quoted by Robert Banks, *Theological Renewal* No. 22, November 1982, p. 18.
13. Ibid., p. 11. NB. John Robinson pleaded for this in 1960 in his book *On Being the Church in the World* (SCM), pp. 83–95.
14. Quoted by Bill Cook, op. cit., p. 15.
15. Taken from a report written by Derek Winter, formerly with the British Council of Churches, describing his visit to Brazil in 1981.

*Chapter 1*

1. The quotations at the beginning of each chapter are taken from

the Vitoria document entitled "The Church the people want" — see Appendix A.
2. Cf. 1 Cor. 16:19; Rom. 16:5.
3. Eg. at Corinth, cf. 1 Cor. 14:23.
4. Eg. at Ephesus, cf. Acts 20:17ff.
5. Robert Banks, *Paul's Idea of Community* (Paternoster, 1980), p. 41. Much of my material on N.T. home churches draws heavily on this stimulating book. His article in *Theological Renewal* No. 22, November 1982, applies his thinking more explicitly to the modern situation.
6. Cf. Acts 2:41–47, 4:4, 5:14, 6:1, 6:7.
7. Acts 4:32.
8. E. F. Schumacher, *Small is Beautiful* (Abacus, 1973), pp. 53–54.
9. Emil Brunner, *The Misunderstanding of the Church.*
10. John Kennedy, *The Days of the Fathers in Ross-shire* (Christian Focus Publications, 1979), p. 81.
11. Ibid., pp. 85–87.
12. Ibid., p. 110.
13. Ian Fraser, *Putting Theology to Work* (Conference for World Mission, 1980), p. 58.
14. Richard Sammon, *Basic Christian Communities: The Portezuelo, Chile, Experience* (Maryknoll Fathers and Brothers, 1982), p. 1.
15. Ibid., p. 15.
16. John Hurston, op. cit., p. 15.
17. Ibid., pp. 16–19.
18. Op. cit., p. 59.


*Chapter 2*
1. Two helpful books, one older and longer, the other more recent and shorter, are: A. B. Bruce, *The Training of the Twelve.* Robert Coleman, *The Master Plan of Evangelism* (Revell, 1963).
2. Matt. 9:36.
3. Eg. John 6:66.
4. Mark 4:1–25, cf. Matt. 13:1–23, Luke 8:4–21.
5. Luke 10:1ff.
6. Luke 6:12ff.
7. John 13:1.
8. Cf. 1 John 3:14; John 13:35, 17:20–23.
9. Mark 9:2ff and 14:32ff.
9a. Eg. John 11:1–46, 12:1–8, Luke 10:38–42, Matt. 21:17, Luke 24:50.
10. John 15:12ff.

11.  Mark 3:13–15.
12.  Eg. Mark 3:31–35.
13.  Phil. 2:5ff.
14.  Quoted by Howard Snyder, *The Radical Wesley* (IVP [USA], 1980), p. 56.
15.  Ibid., p. 36.
16.  James 5:16.
17.  Howard Snyder, op. cit., pp. 59–60.
18.  Ibid., p. 2.
19.  John Wesley, *Works*, vol. VIII, ed. Thomas Jackson (London, 1829–31), p. 254.

*Chapter 3*

1.   Richard Lovelace, *Dynamics of Spiritual Renewal* (IVP [USA], 1979), pp. 162–63.
1a.  Howard Snyder, op. cit., p. 16.
2.   Stanley Ayling, *John Wesley* (Abingdon, 1979), pp. 26–27.
3.   Howard Snyder, op. cit., p. 54.
4.   Ibid.
5.   Ibid., p. 48.
6.   See John Pollock, *Wilberforce* (Lion, 1977), pp. 183–84.
7.   Derek Winter, op. cit.
8.   Ditto.
9.   *Pro Mundi Vita Bulletin* No. 81, p. 13.
10.  Ibid., p. 15.
11.  Howard Peskett, *Asian Challenge 1979* (Publication of Discipleship Training Centre, Singapore), pp. 11–12.
12.  Eileen Vincent, *God Can Do It Here* (Marshalls, 1982), p. 83.

*Chapter 4*

1.   2 Cor. 3:6.
2.   Joao Libanio, *Putting Theology to Work*, p. 29.
3.   Ditto.
3a.  Bill Cook, op. cit., pp. 164–65.
4.   Ibid., pp. 30–36.
5.   K. S. Latourette, *A History of Christianity* (Harper, 1953), p. 1168.
6.   Eph. 4:21.
7.   John 4:24.

8. John 16:13.
9. Quoted by Bill Cook, op. cit., p. 167.
10. Joao Libanio, "A Community with a New Image," *International Review of Mission* No. 68 (July 1979) 271:246–48.
11. The material which forms the substance of the rest of this chapter is drawn from Paul Yonggi Cho's book, *Successful Home Cell Groups* (Logos, 1981).
12. Ibid., pp. 50–51.
13. Ibid., p. 119.
14. Ibid., p. 120.
15. Op. cit., pp. 80–81.
16. Robert Banks, *Theological Renewal* No. 22, p. 16.

*Chapter 5*

1. Eph. 4:1–16.
2. Cf. Isaiah 50:4 and 5, 1 Cor. 14:3, 24–25.
3. Rom. 15:18–24.
4. Eph. 4:16.
5. Eg. Acts 13:1ff.
6. G. Kittel, *Theological Dictionary of the New Testament,* vol. 3 (Eerdmans, 1965), pp. 1035–37.
7. Op. cit., pp. 9 and 10.

*Chapter 6*

1. Cf. Luke 8:18.
2. James Pitt, *Good News to All* (C.I.I.R. and C.A.F.O.D., 1980), pp. 8–9.
3. Robert Banks, *Theological Renewal* No. 22, p. 9.
4. Cf. 1 Cor. 14:40.
5. Eduard Schweizer, *Neotestamentica* (Zwingli, 1963), pp. 338–39.
6. Robert Banks, ditto.
7. Robert Banks, op, cit., p. 11.
8. Quoted by Keith Miller, *Groups that Work* (Zondervan, 1967), pp. 17–18.
9. Quoted by James Pitt, op. cit., pp. 30–31.

*Chapter 7*

1. John Schütz, in the introduction to *The Social Setting of Pauline Christianity* by Gerd Theissen (Fortress, 1982), p. 1.

2. Paternoster 1980, pp. 13–22.
3. *Theological Renewal* No. 22, p. 11.
4. Robert Banks, op. cit., p. 16.
5. For an evangelical critique of the message and impact of Liberation Theology, a helpful book is by Andrew Kirk, *Liberation Theology — An Evangelical View from the Third World* (Marshall, Morgan & Scott, 1979).
6. Derek Winter, op. cit.
7. Attributed to Archbishop Helder Camara of Recife, Brazil.
8. Quoted by Bill Cook, op. cit., p. 246.
9. Ibid., p. 247.
10. Ibid., p. 244.
11. Ditto.
12. Ibid., p. 247.
13. Ibid., pp. 255–57.
14. By Bill Cook, op. cit., p. 243.

*Chapter 8*

1. Joseph Comblin, *The Meaning of Mission* (Orbis, 1977), p. 1.
2. Orlando Costas, *The Integrity of Mission* (Harper & Row, 1979), Intro., pp. xii–xiii.
3. Eg. Mark 1:14–15, Luke 4:43, Acts 1:3 and 28:31.
4. Op. cit, p. 46.
5. Op. cit., p. 47.
6. Eileen Vincent, op. cit., p. 69.
7. Paul Yonggi Cho, op. cit., p. 58.
8. Ibid., p. 59.
9. Ibid., pp. 62–63.
10. Robert Coleman, op, cit., p. 106.
11. Ibid., pp. 117–125.
12. Luke 6:45, Acts 4:20.
13. William B. Lewis, *"The Conduct and Nature of the Methodist Class Meeting"* in *Spritual Renewal for Methodism* ed. Samuel Emerick (Nashville, 1958), p. 25.
14. Paul Yonggi Cho, op. cit., pp. 59–60.
15. Quoted by Bill Cook. op. cit., p. 308.
16. Cf. Rom. 12:13, 1 Tim. 3:2, Tit. 1:8, Heb. 13:2, 1 Pet. 4:9.
17. Eg. Luke 4:38ff, 5:17ff, 5:29ff, 7:36ff, 8:41ff, 10:38ff, 11:37ff, 14:1ff, 19:1ff, 22:7ff, 24:28ff.
18. Matt. 25:35.
19. Rom. 12:9–13.
20. Exod. 17:3 etc.

21.  1 Pet. 4:8 and 9.
22.  Eusebius, *Hist. Eccl.* IV, 15, 14.
23.  G. Kittel, op, cit., vol. V, pp. 20–21.
24.  Eph. 6:12ff.
25.  Quoted by Bill Cook, op. cit., p. 271.

*Chapter 9*

1.  1 Tim. 4:4 and 5.
2.  See W. F. Arndt and F. W. Gingrich, *A Greek-English Lexicon of the New Testament* (University of Chicago Press, 1958), pp. 4–5.
3.  G. Kittel, op. cit., vol. I, pp. 19–21.
4.  Rev. 19:7.
5.  1 Pet. 1:8.
6.  Rom. 12:1.
7.  Col. 3:10–17.
8.  Cf. 1 Cor. 11:26.
9.  Jose Marins, op. cit., p. 67.
10.  Ian Fraser, op. cit., pp. 56–57.
11.  See Bill Cook, op. cit., p. 190.
12.  James Pitt, op. cit., p. 11.
13.  Bill Cook, op. cit., p. 205.
14.  Orlando Costas, op. cit., p. 91.
15.  Heb. 13:8.
16.  Matt. 12:36.
17.  Rev. 8:1.
18.  Cf. Psalm 84:2.

*Chapter 10*

1.  Mark 10:45.
2.  1 John 2:6.
3.  Rev. 3:14–22.
4.  Mark 2:17.
5.  Mark 5:22ff.
6.  Mark 10:17ff.
7.  Mark 10:51.
8.  Mark 2:5.
9.  Mark 10:21.
10.  Luke 19:1–10.
11.  Eph. 5:25.
12.  Ian Fraser, op, cit., p. 55.
13.  John Pollock, op. cit., p. 183.

14.  Cf. Mark 9:35, 10:43–44.
15.  Acts 6:1–7.


*Chapter 11*

1.  Bill Cook. op. cit., p. 1.
2.  Ibid., pp. 468–69.
3.  Ibid., p. 264.
4.  Ibid., p. 273.
5.  Donald Dayton, *Discovering an Evangelical Heritage* (Harper & Row, 1967), p. 73.
6.  Cf. 1 Thess. 5:20–21, 1 Cor. 14:29.
7.  Bill Cook, occasional Essays of the Latin American Evangelical Centre for Pastoral Studies (C.E.L.E.P.), June 1982, p. 70.
8.  James Pitt, op. cit., p. 6.
9.  *Pro Mundi Vita Bulletin* No. 81, April 1980, p. 9.
10.  Richard Lovelace, op. cit., pp. 393–94.
11.  Ibid., p. 157.
12.  Ibid., p. 370.
13.  Quoted by Paul Rees in *The Chicago Declaration* ed. Ronald Sider (Creation House, 1974), p. 79.
14.  Theological Renewal No. 22, p. 10.


*Chapter 12*

1.  Paul Yonggi Cho, op. cit., p. 66.
2.  Ditto.
3.  Ibid., pp. 63–64.
4.  In a personal interview in San Jose in December 1982.
5.  *Basic Christian Communities: The Experience in Portezuelo*, p. 9.
6.  Michael Griffiths, *Get Your Church Involved in Mission* (Overseas Missionary Fellowship), provides many helpful suggestions for such cooperation.
7.  Quoted by Bill Cook, op. cit., p. 27.
8.  Ibid., p. 25.
9.  Jose Marins, interviewed for *East Asian Pastoral Review* 1982, p. 67.


*Chapter 13*

1.  Luke 12:32.
2.  1 Cor. 1:26ff. For interpretations of the social mix in N.T.

churches, see E. A. Judge, *The Social Pattern of Christian Groups in the First Century* (IVP, 1960); and Gert Theissen, *The Social Setting of Pauline Christianity* (Fortress, 1982).

3. Phil. 4:10–13.
4. Cf. p. 76.
5. Richard Lovelace, op. cit., p. 160.
6. Robert Raines, *The Secular Congregation* (Harper & Row, 1968), p. 114.
7. Jose Marins, op. cit., p. 64.
8. Joao Libanio, op. cit., pp. 34–37.
9. See Kathleen Heasman, *Evangelicals in Action* (Geoffrey Bles, 1962), pp. 286–87.
10. James 1:27 (NIV).
11. Luke 1:68.
12. Matt. 25:35 and 42. For other pregnant uses of the same word in the N.T., cf. Acts 7:23, 15:36, Heb. 2:6, Luke 7:16, 1:78, Acts 15:14.
13. G. Kittel, op. cit., vol. II, pp. 599–605.
14. Luke 19:8 and 9.
15. Heb. 13:5 and 16.
16. Acts 20:35.
17. 2 Cor. 8:13–15.
18. Op. cit., pp. 98–99.
19. Gustavo Gutierrez, quoted by Derek Winter.
20. Luke 18:24.
21. Rom. 14:17.
22. G. Kittel, op. cit., vol. V, pp. 871–84. Key references to *parresia* include the following: John 18:20ff, 16:25ff (of Jesus); Acts 4:29, 31, 9:27ff, 18:25ff (of the apostles); 2 Cor. 3:12ff, 2 Cor. 7:4, Philemon 8, 1 Tim. 3:13 (of Christians).

*Chapter 14*

1. Cf. Robert Banks, *Paul's Idea of Community*, Chapter 18 and esp. Appendix on "The Drift of the Pastorals," pp. 192–98.
2. See 1 Cor. 16:15 and 16, where Paul urges the Corinthians to "be subject to" to household of Stephanas and to all "such men", because "they have devoted themselves to the service of the saints."
3. See pp. 98–102.
3a. *Pro Mundi Vita*, op. cit., p. 12.
4. Dr. Pablo Richard, in the course of a personal interview in December 1982.

5. *The Experience in Portezuelo*, op. cit., pp. 4–5.
6. Quoted by Bill Cook, op. cit., p. 395.
7. Howard Snyder, op. cit., p. 63.
8. Quoted by Bill Cook, op. cit., p. 205.

*Epilogue*

1. Interview with Jose Marins, op. cit., p. 65.
2. 2 Cor. 2:15.